GREAT POETS ACROSS AMERICA

A Celebration of National Poetry Month

Brooke Alexander

EDITOR

Washington, D.C.

Great Poets Across America:
A Celebration of National Poetry Month (IV)

Library of Congress
Cataloging in Publication Data

ISBN 978-1-61936-053-2

Printed and manufactured in the United States of America by

2012
To Jamie,

Love you with
all my Heart

Mom ♡

Foreword

For the past sixteen years, poets and poetry have been celebrated every April during National Poetry Month. The Academy of American Poets as well as schools and literary organizations all over the country dedicate this special time to increasing appreciation for poetry in American life and assuring its perpetuality.

As most of you will agree, poetry enriches our everyday life in many ways. It puts us in tune with our surroundings, the environment, current events, and, of course, our own thoughts and feelings. It encourages reflection—something most of us do not take enough time for in today's busy world—and, most importantly, sharing. And this is what National Poetry Month is all about: sharing your time, your poetry, and your artistic visions with others as we work together to spread awareness of poetry across America.

In honor of our poetic heritage, we have compiled this volume of verse to represent today's ever-growing community of amateur poets. Each of you can proudly say you made an active contribution to National Poetry Month 2012, and one that will be read and shared by many. We hope throughout the year you continue to find new, innovative ways to share poetry with others and to encourage others to get involved. Poetry's relevancy in modern culture is attributed to the written legacy of our American poet forefathers. Today, we must keep this art alive and thriving!

Brooke Alexander
Chief Editor

Take My Keys

I know it is too late now.
It could have saved my friend's life with such ease.
If only someone had taken his keys.
He had too much to drink and some doctor gave him the wrong pills.
All he could think about were his many bills.
Looking back, why did no one care enough to take the keys.

Three are dead and he is in a prison cell.
Do not tell me all is well.
To show your love with such ease
Next time, please remember to take his keys.

Brenda Kay Winters

I am a graduate of Texas Tech University (1982), Bethania School of Vocational Nursing (1973), and S. H. Rider High School, Wichita Falls, TX (1971). I worked as a public school teacher, and as a nurse in three states. I am a former home health nurse and maximum security prison officer and jail nurse in Texas. Now I am a retired and disabled American poet and songwriter. "Broken to Mend" was my first recording, although I have written over fifty songs. My parents were murdered in their own home in Texas in 2010, because a felon was appointed as sole caregiver and infiltrated our family and stole most of my parents' life savings. My hobbies are playing piano in nursing homes, gardening, and ballet. I am also an animal lover.

Passing

I read gravestones carved deep
With names of those who weep
In never-ending peace and wonder
If anyone is left to remember
The sound of a voice or look in an eye,
The reasons they laughed or did cry.
Are there friends or family left to say
They lived their lives in a prideful way
Or humbly did on their knees
Ask Heaven's guidance with grateful ease?
Then I wonder when my time is near,
Will there be anyone that will shed a tear
Or when the years have long gone by,
Will someone read my name and sigh
And ask the questions I here have asked?
Will any remember when I have passed?

B. J. McKee

The Six Wishes of the Giraffe

The tall giraffe wanted another tail
Because she did not like the one she had.
She asked for help to the others and the fish said,
Six wishes I can give you, one at a time.
With the elephants I want to play.
Tail of the elephant can you give me?
Poor giraffe with the tail of the elephant,
Nearly she hanged the one going in front.
With fish I want to play.
Tail of the fish can you give me?
Poor giraffe with the tail of a fish,
Nearly she drowns once and for all.
With the monkeys I want to play,
Tail of the monkey can you give me?
Poor giraffe with tail of the monkey,
Hang from the tree, looks like a mango.
With the birds I want to play.
Tail of the bird can you give me?
Poor giraffe with tail of the bird,
In this nest, nearly she doesn't fit.
With the hippos I want to play,
Tail of the hippo can you give me?
Poor giraffe stuck in the mud,
Nothing she has fun this way.
My last wish I am going to use,
To my body, I want to return,
And this way the giraffe learned this time
Nothing is better than who you are.

Ralph Galvan Jr.

Ralph Galvan Jr. *(continued)*

I heard western music on the radio in the forties. I got song books, some in Spanish and in English. I saw that some words in both languages were nearly the same, so it was easy for me to learn Spanish and to also translate all my songs and poems too. Only my mother helped me. When I was a boy, my teacher always asked me to make a drawing for the holidays every year. Mrs. Wakefield was very nice, and a girl loved my drawings, Jean. I used to cut and clean yards near my school with an old push lawn mower the homeowners had in those days. I started to sell a lot of things as a boy. I am a jack of all trades and a notary public from 1965 until May 29, 2013. I was a locksmith in the fifties with used keys and got my diploma in 1996. I have learned a lot of things since a boy just by watching other people. I never had any school for all the things I can do since very young. I lost a drawing I made in 1955 for a contest, but had a negative and one picture made in another state. It was stolen from the post office or state where I sent it. It was in Popular Mechanics and it said "Draw me" on top.

The Dream

Sometimes I wonder
I drift off and dream
I think of this world
And how it all seems.

Anger and pain
Regret and disdain
Power and fear
But one thing is clear:

It lies deep within my heart
And never ceases to grow
My faith ignites the brightest spark
And sheds light wherever I go.

To look is to see
To search is to find
Humility is the key
That can unlock humanity.

You see, we've had it wrong
We were wrong all along:
Thinking of our purpose
By rejecting our creation,
Trying to find the solution
by giving in to temptation.

Our perception has been warped
Our reasoning thrown away
Our paths are being distorted
More and more every day.

Wanting the best of both worlds
But the choice comes down to one
My friend, be sure to choose wisely
Before all is said and done.

Sometimes I wonder
I drift off and dream
Of a faraway land
So pure and serene…

Anna Maria Gabrielli

"The Dream" was inspired by my thoughts and reflections about this world, about how negative and difficult life on this earth can be. However, I know I am never alone because I chose to accept God's love. To know that someone is always beside you, to guide you, to listen to you, to reassure you and ultimately to bless you with infinite love is the greatest comfort of all. Among all of life's uncertainties, the one assurance I hang on to is my faith and trust in my Savior. "For with God nothing shall be impossible." Luke 1:37

Grief and Hope

I was at the nadir of my life
God heard my prayer it seems
For late last night he answered
Jesus brought you to my dreams

I saw Him coming
And I cried for release
I begged him take me with you
He smiled at me and said, Be at peace

He showed me a gift then
A bundle in his arm
Those beautiful eyes I knew
A beautiful smile free of harm

I held my arms out
Tears coursing down my face
He reached for me
The pain was gone, without a trace

Jesus patted my shoulder
He is well cared for, He said with a smile
Don't worry, he will be waiting for you
When you come home in a while

My soul knows peace now
Though my heart feels like stone
I know he is at peace and happy.
I am no longer alone.

Steve Drilling

*This poem was written for my grandson, Atreus Bowman, who died of a rare
condition, approximately thirty days after his birth. I wrote it to help my
daughter. I find it easier to express thoughts and feelings in poetry.*

All My Love

My spirit surges with our life and surely knows its prime.
All reward is yours my wife, I share through all of time.
I love thee, my dear companion, and wonder at God's award—
He gave not a mere fraction, but allowed the entire reward.

I know my role in this time, realizing the better of my dreams.
They take me forth in my prime to solemnly share my schemes.
If I have a humble caring, regardless of its rude source
I'll gladly do the sharing wherever in life's course.

I doubt my immunity lasting as life winds down to end.
While time is spent casting all that's noble, and love's intend.
Alas, the whole of me is set to do with what you will.
Life is often seen with threat, having courage it then to fill.

Together never doubting yet never being content:
Our love to each ne'er flouting, poured out with sweet portent.
The whole of us together with every delight I know;
Our loved ones around us gather to weather what winds might blow.

God has twined our souls with what was cleft before.
We now have common goals and really much, much more.
My spirit surges with our life and surely knows its prime.
All reward is yours my wife, I'll share through all of time.

Garth R. Ashby

This poem was written to my wife of thirty-six years. I am a mechanical engineer by training and profession. However, several of my six granddaughters have introduced me to poetry through their own world. My poetry ranges from serious life reality realization to humorous works about pets, little cock roosters, rodent wars, and tributes to God, life and family members. My philosophy on life, nature, and love of family prompt the more than eighty poems I have written.

Remembering Rex

An old friend whispered to me last night
He said not to worry, not to fright
A gentler breeze distracts my thought
A gust of wind removes distraught
I felt this warm and soothing calm
Another breeze, a waving palm
'Twas then I realized with a smile
He was with me all the while

Joey Dufour

Untitled

Who made this world, who gave it to us?
Sun and sky, oceans and land.
Rain and snow, cold and warm.
Our lives change every second of the day.
You live, person.
Take care of this world.
Let it be happy and beautiful.
Let it be peaceful.
You live, person!
Take care of this world.
Let life be on this world forever!

Sadie Baramikova

I am eleven years old. I live in Canada, in Saint-Catharines, Ontario. I also am in fifth grade in an Online School of America. I go to a Niagara Conservatory of Music. I study piano, violin, and vocal. I go to a dance school called 283 Performing Arts Company. I love to paint, especially oil painting, and ride a bike. My mom is Lamilya Baramikova, I love her with all my heart; she is a nice and gentle woman. I have and love my Aunt Gulnar Yamaldinova, cousin Alexander Yamaldinov and grandma Firuza Baramikova. I love America.

Fire

Flames
Smoke
Heat
Your head spins
How could such a beautiful thing
Be such a tragedy
A restless ball of flame
It can burn
It can heal
It can destroy
It can choose
Fire

Kellie Richardson

Cruelty

One day, I will live in a free land
One day, I won't be bound by these chains
But for now, I have to work shine or rain.

They whip me…they took my family away.
Now they beat me, almost to death, I have to say.

Heaven is a free land where chains are gone,
And I will once again be strong…
No more selling, yelling or crying.
No more market or crying.
No more market places for buying
Slaves like me…

Heaven is a free land with streaming food to eat.
I promise we will never again be beat.
I promise I will see you there someday.
Please listen to our master, promise to obey,
Or you will end up on the death bed like me.
Just because of our color…plain cruelty.

Emalyn Hall

There Is a Window in My Chest

There is a window in my chest
as you look inside you can see my soul.
There are shadows that cloud my eyes
when you look past them you can see the sun.
There are chains around my feet
unlock them and see me run.
There is a hand over my mouth
remove it and listen to what I might say.
There is a smile on my face
do you ever wonder what makes it so?

Lori Sanchez

My love of poetry stems back to childhood. I write today with strong meaning behind my words. This poem is about social justice. I feel everyone should be treated the same and I strive to achieve this in my world. I have grandchildren and I hope the future is kinder to them so they will be kind and loving to all. I hope my words will be understood and felt I want the power of them to be felt into the future.

Know What?

I can hope.
I can pray,
But my life will never be the same.

I will be lost.
I will be afraid,
but there is no hero to save my day.

I am scared and cold,
And I don't want you looking up my nose.

My past is a mystery,
And I don't want people to know
… know … know what?
I don't even know.

All I can say is my life has been hard,
And it still hurts deep inside.
But you wouldn't know.

My laughter hides my screams
my smile; my tears
hugs replaced by high fives
love taken away.

You see…
My past is a mystery,
And I don't want you looking up my nose.
I don't want people to know
… know … know what
I don't even know.

Josephine Cabrera

I started writing last summer and never stopped. Just a few months ago, my teacher had us write a poem for class. It was nothing for me but homework, until I got a letter for publication. I'm glad I started writing. Thank you for telling me I am important. FFF—Faith, Family, Friends.

Emblem of America

Since 1792 A.D.,
The bald eagle, strong, free,
Large, brave, and beautiful will stand
As emblem of our land.
The eagle's nest built high may be
Over land, near seas,
Withstanding storms of awesome might,
Safe from prey day and night.
Stout-hearted mates chosen for life
Share their work, claim their site.
In nests of sticks built high each year,
They hatch chicks without fear.
The bird's defense for any cause
Is its sharp beak and claws,
Nature's way for sustaining life,
Avoiding any rise in strife.
The eagles, beautiful in flight
Through gift of long-range sight
Can see what lies on earth below,
Alert for food or foe.
Stern eyes, yellow beak, and head white
Add stature to great might.
God, grant our emblem and land be
Ever safe, strong, and free!

Hulda K. Sellingsloh

My aim in life has been to be a force for good. Since childhood, I have had many talents for art and poetry. After being a busy attorney, wife, and mother of four children, I began painting at age fifty. I received a commission to paint a large image of the bald eagle from a retired army officer and was reminded that the

bald eagle is an emblem of our country. I now hope to make known or remind people and especially students of its distinctive traits and beauty. As I approach my one-hundredth birthday on November 29, 2012, I still enjoy writing poetry, painting, reading, and shopping for colorful clothes. I now submit my poem, "Emblem of America," with hopes that it will be accepted to give great tribute to nature's plan honoring a great nation, America.

Salute to the Copy Editor

'Twas the night before deadline and all through the house
Not a creature was stirring, except for my mouse.
Fixing commas and colons as fast as I can
Inserting conjunctions like "if," "but," or "and."
Check for spelling and tenses—one final run-through
Indentations and titles; I think that will do.
And just when I thought the end was near
What to my wondering eyes appear?
Eight tiny ellipses, all in a row
My goodness, but five of them have to go!
Em dash away now, the end is in sight
It's time to exclaim to all a good night!

Grace E. Baker

The Painter's Rise

The darkness, it plagues the earth.
Only the King could save.
He chose a brush to paint rebirth
To combat the dragon, who our souls crave.
The dragon, that old serpent
Consuming the planet, a sinful feast,
Only failing to conquer the repent.
A fool, ignore the beast.
The King, He is coming!
Covering creation, a glorious revival.
With the eye He watched, now paints the running.
Master Artist, You are able!
In the hills, they meet,
The Creator prevailing the liar.
To the abyss, the beast in defeat.
Above the King, there is none higher!
To the sky! The love came down,
A tidal wave of glory with no opposition.
The banished beast again is drowned.
Hail the King! The repent, the Christians!
But the beast will return as the Son will set,
And we shall withstand, for the eye is watching.
In the stronghold, we sing to the inglorious wretch,
Behold, oh, night! The Son forever coming!

Matthew C. Shaw

This poem was written while on an early morning flight to Honduras. I was flying there on a mission's trip to assist the people of La Ceiba. I looked over the mountains, watching the sunrise breaking the dawn. The scene drew me to an image of God. In John 8:12, Jesus says, "I am the light of the world. Whoever will follow me will never walk in darkness, but will have the light of life." The darkness of sin has confusion, pain, and suffering, but God is greater and conquers sin so that we may have eternal life.

Growing Up

When I was younger,
I thought the world was full of good,
And everyone got their happy endings.
But as I got older,
I began to see just how wrong I was.
I learned that the world wasn't
Filled with good,
That there was some bad.
I learned that the number of happy endings
Was decreasing every day.
I'm older now than I was before.
Now I think that there is more bad in the world than good.
I believe that happy endings
Are only for the lucky few,
And I keep wishing that everything
Was like I thought it was
When I was three,
But wishing won't get me very far
In this world, will it?

Emily Harris

This poem shows my frustration with the way the world is today. It shows feelings of hopelessness. Poetry has become a major part of my life, though I've only been writing for less than a year. I write whenever I can as often as I can. Ideas just seem to flow from the pencil, and on paper, it turns into eighty-some poems and short stories I've written. I love to write, but I love those close to me even more. I'm only sixteen, but I know that I'll be writing for the rest of my life.

Falling In Love

How beautiful the twinkling stars,
How beautiful the moon;
The cool night air hums along
A bewitching but silent tune.

If you drink the moon's elixir,
Moon babies will dance around your heart.
Before you can blink an eye,
Feel the pangs of true love start.

A honeysuckle breeze
Will take your breath away;
Drink the moonbeams in the water.
Love will surely come your way.

Stardust will fall upon your hair,
On every rock and flower.
Love will blossom everywhere,
And sweeten your heart by the hour.

When the day comes to an end,
You will bask in love's desire.
It will surely touch your soul,
And set your heart on fire.

JoGene Vega

I am a sixty-five-year-old wife, mother and proud grandmother of six wonderful grandchildren—a seventh munchkin is on the way. Since childhood, I have loved writing poetry as a hobby. A poem is a fingerprint from the heart. I also love to draw, paint, write songs and have been working on my first novel for the

JoGene Vega *(continued)*

last three years. I also love cooking and gardening and realize I can't function without inspiration and creativity in my life. I find poetry to be a beautiful form of therapy and expression. I believe it can help build our faith and our love. It stirs the fire deep within and soothes the soul; it can give you comfort and purpose. You can express your deepest yearnings, joys and sorrows. It gives you a sense of accomplishment and helps our essence and imaginations soar. Poetry can be dynamic, melodious, comforting, shocking, mysterious, passionate, comedic, tragic, and it encompasses all of life's ups and downs. It helps you appreciate the beauty of life and the elegance and power of words—poetry helps awaken the spirit.

Unknown

I can't see you in
the night sky,
I hear you in the moonlight
when the stars are bright.
You can't see me
I'm in front of you.
You can hear me when
the moonlight is blue.
When you talk to me I
feel free,
just as I see you my soul flies.
My heart pounds very fast
when I hear you smile.
While your touching me
I feel happy.
Every time you're away from me
I can't understand the way it feels.

Samantha Chandler

To tell you the truth, this was the very first poem I ever wrote. I wrote it in ninth grade, because I just wanted to express myself to a guy. I honestly think of my past when I think of "Unknown" and the way I got treated from a guy friend about three years ago; he just wanted a few things I couldn't give to him.

The Carousel

I hear the music it's calling my name,
So many horses, but no two the same.
All dressed up in their bright shiny colors,
And let's not forget all of the others.

"Hey, Mr. Rabbit, can I please have a ride?"
"Welcome my child, please step inside."
Each will take you away through the air.
To places unknown while you are there.

Watching the animals dance on the wind,
Never wanting the ride to end.
Taking me back to carefree days.
Leaving me in a childhood haze.

Round and round, up and down, all the animals go
Funny, how when you hop on their backs, it never seems to
grow old.
For we who remain a child at heart,
Only the carousel can fill that part.

So dance pretty horses, dance for me
Then I will go and let you be.
Feel the joy; it's a wonderful thing,
Oh! My goodness; I grabbed the brass ring.

Teresa L. Haley

Growing up and still today, my favorite ride is the carousel. It is all about hopping on the back of one of the animals and having an adventure that is mine alone. Each one brings a different joy and adventure and no two are alike. I find such joy in the experience. Oh, yes, if you happen to grab the brass ring that is a ride you will never forget...I hope I never grow old.

My Life

My vision for the future:
Search through my adventures
And identify all my troubles.
It's a priority, for sure.

I thank God for my family,
What a beautiful destiny.
Having my three wonderful daughters,
A unique son that I cherish,
A wife whom I love—
Such a precious dove.
Regardless of all my problems,
I enjoy writing my poems.

I have seen precious moments,
Times that I'll never forget.
Regardless of all the torments
There is always a pretty sunset.

Life always continues
As the time defines;
Keep living your values
Today, tomorrow, and always.

Geronimo Aguirre

I'm a Mayan-Kanjobal of Guatemala. I left my homeland when I was seventeen years old, due to a civil war. I lived in Mexico for a while and eventually came to the U.S.A. and became a U.S. citizen in 2000. I have done various farm jobs and construction work; I presently work for Schwan's Food, making frozen pizzas. I have been married for almost thirty years and have four kids: three daughters and one son. I also have one grandkid. My poem, "My Life," is a dedication to my family, with great appreciation. I like being a handyman, landscaping, painting, traveling, reading, writing and playing golf. Poems are great therapy, as they release the daily pressures of life!

Clouds

Have you ever had the privilege
Among the clouds to fly?
To forget those things that bother you
In the freedom of the sky?

So often people speak of clouds
As obscuring the brightness of day:
Or think of others in relationship
To storms that come their way.

But when you fly above the clouds
And behold the beauty there
You think not of the storms that beat,
Nor of your earthly care.

Behold a sight that fills with awe,
Revealed to you in softest white—
Towering clouds that stand so tall,
Fleecy forms in majestic flight.

Alvin L. Barker

As a licensed pilot, in 1966 I flew from Liberal, KS to Big Spring, TX to take our children, Ken and Kathy Barker, to see their Scott grandparents. At takeoff, it was quite cloudy. Upon flying through the cloud layer and arriving above it, the sight was amazing. Below, a carpet of white clouds, above which were about 200 feet of clear space, then above that a ceiling of white clouds. Between were pillars of clouds that went from carpet below to ceiling above, reminding me of pillars on a building. They were relatively round and maybe 100 feet in diameter, but with open space to fly.

Angels

You meet me here.
I meet you now.
We breathe this second.
Our deserted hearts taste the present.
Angels might appear.

Our skin leading the way.
My heart is drumming.
You breathe to my beat.
We break open.
Angels are hearing.

Tears of uncertain liberty,
vibrating with your pulse.
Water drops landing on my chest,
you are drinking me.
Angels are here.

Our bare naked souls visible,
for us to seize.
Entangled in our mold,
we reach above the ceiling.
Angels are beaming.

Lips traveling uncovered terrain.
Rising love to come undone.
Fingers finding secrets.
Our hearts soar.
Angels are near.

I give you me.
You give me you.
Boundless night of us.
We know freely.
Angels are here.

Kristina Hall

Kristina Hall *(continued)*

I was born in Sweden and moved to the USA in 1992. I live in Chicago with two teenage sons and visit Sweden several times a year. I will always have one foot in each country. I am a freelance writer and my work is in both English and Swedish. My poetry is my heart talking.

Ivy's Kingdom

The park sign read "No admittance after dark"
But her home was here within this park
When the sun surrendered to wear a widow's veil
The rusty gates were locked as if in a prison's cell
She tied the ancient lock, guardian of the gates
And with a click of sound, she entered her estate
Wandering to a lamppost that for years had shown no light
She hid within the shadows in case of need of flight
Overtaken by nature, near a creek that served her baths
She had discovered an old park bench upon a forgotten path
She laid yesterday's news as a blanket for her throne
Then sat and viewed her kingdom that she called her home
She felt cold; she shivered, pulling newspaper to her chest
Then with a sigh of surrender, she laid her head to rest
Her dreams were of the warmth of summer, a bonfire on the beach
But dreams cannot deliver life's simple need for heat
Found frozen as the iron statues after many mornings passed
No one had been looking, no one cared to ask
Where is Ivy, the park lady? Where could Ivy be?
I'll answer that one for you—abandoned, left to freeze

Pamela S. Ray

The poem "Ivy's Kingdom" was inspired by a homeless woman whom I encountered while visiting one of the East Coast's wealthiest resort areas. I was appalled by the number of elderly Americans that were left to fend for themselves regardless of dire circumstances or an inability to do so. We cannot ignore a past generation that literally fought to ensure that America would remain the land of the free. May God have mercy on the souls of these forgotten Americans, and may they find warmth, nourishment, and shelter. Most of all, let them be showered with human compassion.

Savannah

Savannah in the springtime is so wondrously green.
The flowers, all blooming, make a magnificent scene.
The azaleas and camellias, the magnolias and more,
Savannah, the great lady, with her gifts to adore.
Savannah in the summertime, she's really getting hot.
The beach can get crowded, so hurry to get a good spot.
The Atlantic roars and rolls, splashing waves sky high,
Savannah, a playful girl, by no means is she shy.
Savannah in the autumn is so easy to take in.
The river with a marshy breeze that twists and turns in the wind.
The air is crisp and clear, the temperature is just right,
Savannah at her very best, she's such a marvelous sight.
Savannah in the winter is special and quite rare.
Sometimes she's very cold, but most times, she doesn't dare.
There are times as late as Christmas
When short sleeves can be worn,
Savannah in all her majesty and seasonal treasures adorn.

Pamela Howard-Oglesby

I am a native of Savannah, GA, a handicapped individual, legally blind from birth. By education and training, I am a licensed mortician, but I most enjoy volunteer work acting as a community activist and organizer. I'm co-author of a book entitled Savannah's Black First Ladies, Volume I, a collection of stories of African-American female firsts locally here in Savannah, Chatham County. It is being used to work with young girls and women to empower and encourage them. Savannah's weather is wonderful almost all year around. People come to Savannah for its history and weather.

God's Love

Here I lay, a hopeless mass of clay
Dirt on every human's way
A waste that no one wants to play
Helpless, doomed for misery.
You came at a very timely moment
When no one dares to hug
You stretched Your hand, touched my face
Your eyes envisioned love.
Without any sense of certainty
Your arms wrapped my being
Your love filled with compassion
In my soul ignited hope and essence.
With tears flowing down my cheeks
I laid my head on Your bosom
I felt a total sense of security
And an awesome fire of dawn!

Adelfa G. Lorilla

This poem was written when I was meditating on God's goodness in our lives, how He took our family from the "miry clay and set our feet upon the rock"—Him! We were very poor in the Philippines, lots of hardships and struggles, but God brought us to America and changed our way of living! I praise and thank Him for my precious husband, Ricardo, our eight children (Karen, Jan, Zheena, Andrei, Armi, May, Ric, and Jesse), seven grandchildren, and four adopted ones. They are God's channel of love, my strength, my joy. To God be the glory!

The Dream, the Promise, the Confession

Thirty years, a thousand miles apart in time and space,
The lovers rush to reconnect in life's most desperate race.
She flies to him, he waits for her,
Time's endless moments wait,
Each longing for the other's arms to wrap in love's embrace.
She lands, he's there.
They touch at last.
The clock and time stand still.
They feel as if no time has passed.
Love feels new and always will.
These lovers know a love so strong, not measured like the rest
For them apart at weakest point, together, at their best.
How will it end, this lovers' race, strong feelings seal their fate.
She begs of him, "Hold fast, my love."
Joy comes to those who wait.

Lori L. Robinson

Inspiration—everything, whenever and wherever I may find it.

Responsibility

I'm the only one responsible for my behavior.
I feel no need for a human savior.
To control my destiny, I desire.
If I said anything else, I'd be a liar.
There's no one else I can control.
Even the thought is exceedingly droll.
I always do as well as I can,
And try not to hassle woman or man.
I've done some things that did not make me proud,
Sometimes inconsiderate, occasionally loud,
But over all, I'm pleased with the way I am,
And to deny my belief would be a sham.
Many things I have done have made me glad,
And I deeply cherish the good times I've had.
I've learned as much as I could from life,
Including the benefits as well as the strife.
A certain principle keeps coming through.
So often I encounter it, it must be true.
I'm the only one responsible for what I do.
The world would be better if others adopt that philosophy too.

Maurice Levy

I am an emeritus professor of pediatrics and an associate dean for faculty development at the Medical College of Georgia. I have published over one hundred professional articles, books (two), and poems. All of my poetry relates to issues that I feel are very important to my life. I'm sure that anyone reading my poetry can feel my passion for the subject. My first wife of fifty years, Loris Levy, passed away in 2005. I currently have been married one year to Michelle Kamet Levy. I have three children, Arden L. Levy, MD, Andrea H. Levy, MD, and James M. Levy, MD. I was diagnosed with pancreatic cancer in 2008. I was given at the most two years to live. I am still here and cancer-free five years later. I totally cherish my life.

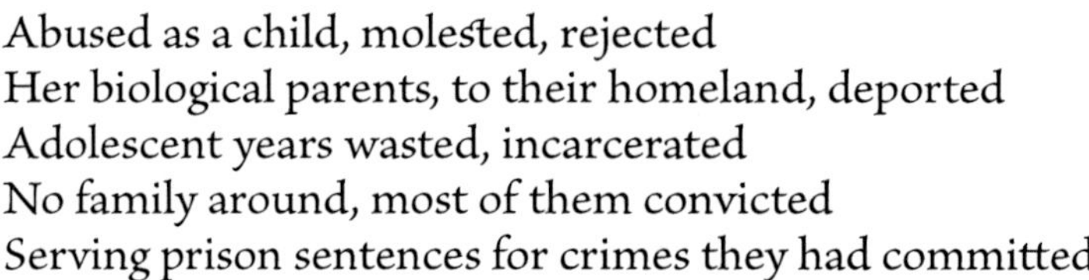

Recovered, Renewed, Restored!

Abused as a child, molested, rejected
Her biological parents, to their homeland, deported
Adolescent years wasted, incarcerated
No family around, most of them convicted
Serving prison sentences for crimes they had committed

As a young adult, she turned to prostitution
She needed the money to feed her drug addiction
Her binging, partying, excessive alcohol consumption
Lying, stealing, with no sense of conviction
Were leading her deeper in sin and self-destruction

She had several trials with cohabitation
Then married someone; it was mere infatuation
The first six months were like being on vacation
Had beautiful flowers, lots of loving attention
Until the day she was beaten beyond recognition

Kicked, punched, slapped, terrorized
Battered, bruised, burnt, scarred for life
Embarrassed, humiliated, in pain agonized
Dreams shattered, life threatened, demoralized, traumatized
She couldn't dare retaliate; took the blows like a child

She felt powerless, helpless, hopeless, depressed
The thought of leaving the house was adding to her stress
She had no food, no money, no other place to stay
She felt guilty about the thought of running away
And felt she couldn't survive for a single day

She is now grateful to God that she is a survivor
And studying to become a Social Worker
No more a victim; been redeemed, made clean
She recovered from a life of sin and shame
Feel renewed in Christ, it's no longer a dream
And restored in the family of the Heavenly King

Rhoda Benjamin

Rhoda Benjamine was born in the United Kingdom and grew up in Grenada, West Indies. She currently resides in Huntsville, AL. Her professional background is in nursing with a specialization in behavioral health. She is a clinical instructor at the College of Nursing, University of Alabama, Huntsville. She is married with one daughter and acknowledges God as the Giver of her poetic gifts. Her work of poetry started about four decades ago and has predominantly been of the traditional style. This poem is an abridged version of the original poem written upon request for the "Woman Helping Women Recover" Convention, at her local church in March 2012.

Falling No More

Falling, falling, someone catch me
Before I hit the ground
Sensation, temptation, fire surrounds me
No one makes a sound
Crying, screaming, begging forgiveness
Wanting badly to be found
Hopeless, helpless, no one hears me
The winner has been crowned

Fighting, biting, clawing to the top
My deception and lies make my mound
Desperate, abandoned, the darkness falls in
It feels like millions of pounds
Sorrow, angst, my attempts are futile
No one cares at all
Wishing, musing, faintly wondering
How far did I fall?

A sudden light, I take His hand
My savior, standing tall
Flying, soaring, high above the clouds
Faint voices, distant calls
Hope, faith, He gives me strength
I'm not alone at all
Falling, falling, He catches me now
I never fall
I'm saved

Arika L. Craig

Whispers of Home

Azure ocean currents rush up,
Reaching out to greet my saddened tears.
One straggling thought in mind—
What if time stopped here and froze?
Remained framed in the moment
Miraculous in articulate shades
Of the most royal gold and deepest blue
In the moment where color never fades.
I slowly sift my fingers
Through the seemingly fragile sand.
Clouds floated by in a daze,
Configuring shapes I couldn't comprehend.
Echoing, crashing upon the rocks
Was the only sound to break silence.
I want to live here forever
In this place that never renders violence.
A reverie where peace was found
In every ripple of a wave,
And love was held in such capacity,
Not one wall had ever gave.
But against my deepest wishes,
I know I must leave and venture home,
So I'll hold my heart close to me
While my soul remains to roam.
Glancing up, I capture the sun
In the one fragment of radiant fire
And the moon following close behind
Running the eternity race where neither tire.
The sun with gold and red beauty
Will always manage to win,
For light forever overcomes darkness,
And this is where time truly did begin.
A fluttering smile etched on my face
Until it spread to my eyes of blue turned gray.
I know not to shed a tear or worry
Because I will soon return another day
While my feelings, wishes, and dreams will never stray.

Sierra N. Butcher

The Pain Also Rises

Enduring life with so many sorrows
Everlasting memories of disorders
The disconnection of family and friends
It feels like rain pouring out of the past
All so perfectly there in its place
Encouraging as it progresses endlessly
Rising to higher heights on a journey
As painful as it seems to have no hurt
All the bitterness yet seemingly so sweet
How it is so real and not to be defeated
As the pain also rises

Tyrone Glessner

War

Buildings destroyed and homes ablaze with broken down doors,
Bombs rattle the earth, cars on fire, victims praying for no more.
Rubble covers the ground, black and grey smoke all around.
Gunfire and bullets fly across the sky, decaying bodies piled high.
Havoc and chaos everywhere, screams and cries are what you hear.
Feeling lost and afraid, faces of panic and despair.
Hunger and famine spread throughout the land.
Friends embrace and hold each other's hand.
Mothers and fathers clutch their children's limp bodies.
Others search for their friends and family.
Children roam the streets all alone, weeping with fear.
There are countless victims of warfare.
How many more victims will there be?
When will this fight for power cease?
How did human life become so insignificant?
When will the terror end, for humans' sake?
Power? Control? Ignorance. Heartless war!

Marisol A. Reyes

Our Own Little World

To you and your New Year's resolution,
May it do you good.
Another year has gone by.
Another year is yet to come.
Day by day we live our lives
Caught in our own little world around us,
Not daring to venture outside
Our own little comfort zone we have come to know.
Do not ask us any questions that may make us think.
Do not make any demands upon us.
We do not want to know what is going on around us.
Just leave us alone and let us go our own way,
For we are scared or this new outside world
Full of different people, different ideas
With a way of life we do not know,
Creeping into our backyard of our own little world.
What will happen to us
If we venture outside our own little world?
By intermingling with these new people and trying out new ideas,
Will we make fools of ourselves
Or will we just disappear altogether,
Or maybe by opening our hearts and doors
To new people and ideas,
We will make new friends, have confidence,
And feel better about ourselves,
And our little world will become a better world to live in,
And we will not have to be scared of this new world anymore.
To you and your New Year's resolution,
May it do you good.
Another year has gone by.
Another year is yet to come.

Deborah A. Fogel

I was born and raised in the countryside of Pennsylvania, what is now called Jacobsburg State Park. My parents are Richard and Betty Werkheiser. I have one brother and three sisters. We grew up to be a very close-knit family with a love and respect for nature. I grew to love poetry when I read Robert Frost's poems as a child. To me, poetry is much like a walk in the woods; it has a calming effect and soothes my soul.

For a Sinner

Sometimes I feel we don't deserve
God's mercy, His love and grace,
And that we haven't done enough
To earn that higher place.
But that's the beauty of His love
And why He sent His son
To pay a price for who we are,
All sinners, and I am one.
As we greet each bright new day
And to see His morning star
Brightly shining in the sky,
My God, how great Thou are.

Dusty C. Duty

Answers

It keeps me up at night,
Longing and hoping and crying
For the right words to say.
Why does it have to be this way?
Who is to blame?
I pray and pray,
But the answers don't come my way.
So I wait for someone
To give my mouth the words
To give my heart the trust
And to give my mind the rest.
Why must I carry on this way?
Am I to blame?
I pray and pray
Answers, please hurry my way.
It's not for lack of trying
Not knowing what to do has me dying
And I still can't understand
Why these words have to be said.
Maybe it doesn't have to be this way
Maybe no one is to blame
I still pray and I still pray
I think the answers are coming my way.

Emily Scroggins

Nightmares and Dreams

Darkness falls across my bed
My eyes close once again
There in the dark you lie
Images seen I wish I had forgotten
Not meant to forget So why do I still dream
Dreams are a never ending void
A beginning an ending
To a suffering world
They will not let you forget
Let you lose yourself
Not if you're not meant to
Are they your subconscious
Are they your hopes
Or maybe a wish made by your heart
But who would wish so much pain
Who would want to dream of pain
Pain that only hurts the dreamer
Maybe they aren't dreams at all
Maybe they are the opposite
Nightmares, nightmares are the black hole of a dreamworld
Some would say frightening others would say troubled
But is a person having a nightmare troubled or are they simply in pain
Is a nightmare there to simply make you remember
I try to forget, I try to move on, I try to heal
I try I try but I can't
I see nightmares as a punishment
They punish you by scaring you
Making you feel pain
Pain you've already felt while awake
Nightmares make it impossible to escape
To escape problems

Love loss betrayal the passing of a loved one
The loss of a best friend
The loss of a true love
Nightmares and dreams both can cause pain
Both can cause suffering but can they be the first
The first to cause a loss
A loss of a person's sanity
Yes

Kayla Dudley

Thoughts of You

Thoughts of you,
Singing thoughts
Rhythmically moving through my mind.
Forest's sunrays
Streaming down in gold dust
Upon your face.
Warm smiling lips kiss its warmth.
Garden song hummingbird.
Thoughts of you
Whirling around my head.
Wind breezes shaking loose
Memories of you embraced with wings.
Rainbow's colors
Painted across the blue sky
Reached to touch my hand,
Magically disappearing.
Thoughts of you,
Soft, rich brown earth,
God's chair to rest upon.
Golden leaves falling,
God's rain of colors and shapes.
Restful, graceful, river flowing,
Washing, cleansing the soul.
Eyes bathed in soft, white lacy form.
Thoughts of you.

Carole Saleh

Written in memory of Lori Jean Harkson, the daughter of my dear, loving sister, Sharon Louise Harkson and Skip, her daddy. We all share the loving memory of a young, beautiful soul, our dear Lori Jean. For you all.

Strawberries in the Sun

Why should we live in a limited world
Watching others at play?
Why should we live in a limited world
Where life is just a breath away?
Rich heritage belongs to all,
Its legacy for everyone
To be what you were meant to be,
And gather strawberries in the sun.
Why should we live in a limited world
Where life is just a step away,
And wish to soar the hills in love,
Waiting for a brighter day?
Rich heritage belongs to all,
Its legacy for everyone
To be what you were meant to be,
And gather strawberries in the sun.
Let's start a day that will last forever
So little ones and big ones too
Can giggle and have some fun,
And gather strawberries in the sun.

Joan P. Bassett

I consider myself a contemporary poet. In my poetry, I write about living in a better world, our spiritual side, and draw attention to causes, such as the homeless and our veterans' sacrifices, especially. I do wish to bring a joyful noise through poetry. I also write in other genres.

Here to Show Us the Way

Jesus was born on Christmas Day
Asleep in a manger on a mattress of hay
His birth was made known by a shining star
That could be seen both near and far
Here to deliver peace and love
Jesus truly was a gift from Heaven above
Let us celebrate His arrival on this day
For He was born to show us the way

Sierra Plys

When I wrote this poem, my intent was to reach the lost so that they would know the only way to salvation. I hope my writing inspires you to love Jesus and let Him show you the way.

Defy

Stretching out over the dual mind
 I can feel a bad emotion
From worry and shame
 Came this feeling

Is it of the guilt that lie within
 We will never know
Is it of the shame of a love gone
 We will never see again
Is it just misery
 Your life is energy-less

Nothing is something that misery likes

Something is not nothing
But something to find to defy misery

I see a hope.

Aretha Boyd

I am from Lake Village, AR—a very small town filled with great mentors. I have three children, Stephen, Taylor Joshua, Tiya, who inspire me to write. My poem is about some things I have gone through in my lifetime, by looking in on the world and its many surprises for life. This is just one of many poems I've written over the years. I love this one the most because I believe there is a hope for people; even if the road that you travel has rough spots that you don't understand, just remember to defy and find hope.

Flickers in the Night

Night rolls in from a beautiful orange sunset.
It rolls a blanket of darkness void of starlight with a faint glimmer
from a quarter moon.
Through the darkness there are flickers of light.
First one then two as the night moves on.
More and more flickers have begun.
The flickers are the slender lightning bugs.
They fly by as though floating lightning throughout the night.
Always hoping to find others to bond with in their flight.
To watch them is quiet tranquil as they flicker through the night.
They blink out little symphonies as they light up the trees.
What unique little creatures these lightning bugs indeed.
They light like little beacons as soon as they take flight.
Call them mini Cessna's that fly throughout the night.,
So when you see those flickers moving through the night.
Remember the little lightning bugs shining their little lights.

Patina V. Waters

I am a native Washingtonian and a mother of one child, Robert. I love reading, movies, writing and volunteering. My inspirations come to me sometimes like lightning in a bottle. This is a blessing and an honor to be able to share my poetry with others.

Moment of Inspiration

I am one with all-that-is,
Neither greater nor lesser than,
But equal partner and co-creator.

I touch the sun, moon and stars
And they touch me.
I am the leaves of the tree of life
As well as its fragrant blossoms
And the orchestra of the wind.

I breathe the essence of divinity.
It's nectar fills my mouth
And I, myself, am the wine of love.

My self whirls with ancient rhythms
And leaps with the joy of beingness.
The breath of God fills me
In this moment of eternal cycles.

My soul is my coat of many colors.
It is woven with textures of my many lives
And spins as a sacred wheel
Creating one new color,
Creating one new verse of God.

Diane Crawford

From the time I was a child, I have sensed the invisible within our lives. My poetry reflects my inner perception.

Dark to Light

Black, twisted claws of the forest surround you. The only light you see
is from the sick, full moon, taking joy in your misery. You can feel the
ruby eyes of a raven watching, counting out steps until you fall off the
    beaten path.
Bones softened, sulked skin, muscles weakened, you see your own
    image transform.
First: Buddha with a belly and bald head to match.
Next: you see a Buddhist monk, quiet, and preserved, aware of chaos in
    your body.
Now: brittle, ghost-like, a walking carcass with a strong heart stares
    back at you.
Looking around, you feel as if the trees are moving, inching closer,
    reaching out.
"Is there anymore use? Should I continue on this broken ground
beneath my feet, or give up, and stop here?" the question burns in your
    mind, repeating over, over and over.

Pushed by the wind, stumbling over your feet, a hand catches you. It
is warm, comforting. Its light touch helps you to your feet. Pressing its
lips to your ear. "Don't you give up."
A hooded figure of a woman-face hidden in black, flowing garbs, fitted
from head to toe fills your sight. You spot the lantern swinging in her
other hand-she parts her lips, "You see this light? It is your flame of
Hope. As long as you trust in it, it will never go out, nor will it fail.
Side by side, the lantern leading the way out of the wicked forest-the
woman reminds you. You are not alone. You never were, and you never
will be. Your flame is fueled by the hope of everyone who holds you in
their heart, and prays for you every night.

One step at a time, maybe a stumble here and there, but soon will you
come out of this damn forest.

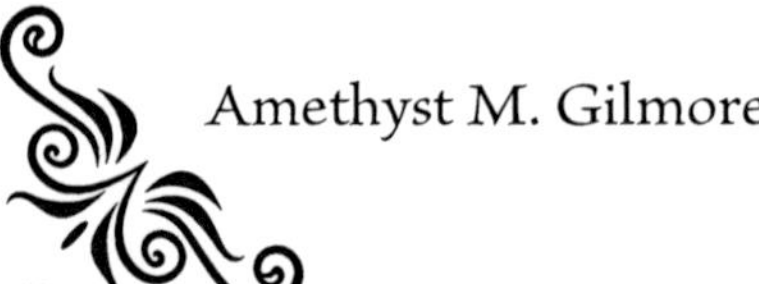

Amethyst M. Gilmore

I wrote "Dark to Light" for my Tio Paco who is currently undergoing cancer. It was just a little pick-me-up idea I had for Christmas, but everyone who has read it says it is inspiring and places a smile on their face after a bad day. We all have our ups and downs, but soon we'll found our way out of the forest. I'm only eighteen years old, so I still have a lot to learn about writing, but I hope that more will be out in the world and reach out to people.

Fooling All of the Fools

But what they say be harassed is the weak?
Fools know not all of me.
For, all the petulant bitter fools seeks,
love is all they wish not to see.
Let them speak their croaked myths and lies.
Prove them wrong with beauty's eyes.
I will rip my flesh and scar my bones,
burn my hands to unthinkable tones.
Those fools who fake happiness use others as a toy.
They lost themselves and never found joy.
Happiness is okay when life goes good,
but those with joy stayed "happy" even when disappointment stood.
Some understand while others will not.
These facts will linger around time more than not.
If we can survive the frayed ends of this beginning,
the strong bond of us later with award us an ending.
Life is just something we live.
Love is just something we feel.
A heart surges life into us.
At least time can heal a heart.
A brain has let us down with so many destructive thoughts.
Maybe the brain has fooled the weakest fool.

Sondie Rae Capps

I am quite a young poet. I have had some hard times in my life and experienced tough situations. Although not many people were there for me, poetry always was and still is. Most of the time writing poetry was not only my own little way to escape but it was more like a friend to talk to. As long as I had a pencil and a scrap sheet of paper, I felt safe.

Major Devilleres

Major Devilleres, what a hero,
My, oh, my.

Major Devilleres, what super human powers,
Watch that hero fly.

He stands for justice and does what is right.
He battles evil both day and night.

Major Devilleres, what a protector is he
When fighting for justice and liberty.

End?

David L. Devilleres

I created "Major Devilleres" to carry on my name, long after I am gone. Major Devilleres is an immortal superhero, whose feats of bravery should live on. My name is David L. Devilleres, and "Major Devilleres" was created in my mind. Major Devilleres' duties are just this: to battle evil by fighting crime. P.S. I am writing other poems about Major Devilleres; I would like to put them in a book someday. I am retired and a poetry lover. I am sixty-five years old. I would also like to write short stores on our hero, Major Devilleres. Perhaps one day...

Rainbow Butterfly

As I gather to my vibrations, the essence of love and light,
I am surrounded by heavenly scents of rose, incense and myrrh.
A shimmering, quivering, exquisite Rainbow Butterfly in flight—
Encompassing me, entering into my heart deep within.

I feel myself being born anew, as I expand with love
Given freely, warmly, gently. With compassion to me
From the Godhead Holy Trinity, Jesus the Christ all above
So I might gather their essence around and in my consciousness.

I send you, crystal rainbow moonbeams, love's potion,
From my secret heart or their perfect, purest Love.
Within the myriad layers of my complex emotions
Dwells the effervescent, eternal spark given by God above.

As you go about your daily life, no matter day or night—
Be you at work, rest or play, dreaming or asleep—
If perchance you see a glimmering multihued, lovely light
Remember 'tis the God essence of a rainbow of love in flight.

As you awake each glorious morn to sunny, sunbright
Send someone you know, confused or sad, a rainbow of many hues
Permeated by God's essence of warm compassionate light—
A shimmering, quivering, Rainbow Butterfly, love in flight.

Rev. Burdetta Siefken

*Hello, I believe I (and everyone) have angels and spirit guides during this lifetime.
One of mine is named Rainbow Butterfly; I feel it is sent by the Holy Spirit of God
to help guide me here. God the Creator is so much more than we give Him credit
for—all-knowing, capable of all and everything , creator of our world, universe,
and all others existing now and still being formed. I thank God, my parents, my
husband (deceased), my angels and guides, Jesus the Way Shower, for my
life, my experiences here and many varied life-lessons—some yet
to be learned.*

Yonder the Hills (Passing of the Storm)

With a crying heart, weeping soul
yonder did I climb
wading through the muddy waters
sailing amongst the stormy weather
I believe…I knew. I felt…
A longing to taste the sweet nectar
of spiritual resurrection
to soar amongst the heavens on a
wing and a prayer…
To penetrate the walls of Jericho
with a spear, molded of mine tribulations
to arise…new, refreshed…
to sip on the wine of uplifted in a
crystal goblet, sparkling of mine tears…
mine cries, "Oh! Alas." I
walked the blistering sands of the desert…
East…Africa… Jerusalem…
Jordan…to cross that final bridge…
Yonder those hills through the storm
Home! Home! There's no place
like home…with you, a diamond
Encrusted vow of sacred testament…
I am here…I have arrived…

F. Le Vonier Aldridge II

I have been a writer since the youthful age of eleven years old, and my greatest inspiration has been the memoirs of Edgar Allan Poe along with the renowned W. E. B. Dubois. I am creatively influenced by the prolific era of the Harlem Renaissance. I am a playwright, screenwriter, actor, and a watercolor artist in the realm of abstract (theatrical masques) with intimate colours of pastel shades.

F. Le Vonier Aldridge II *(continued)*

I feel I am brilliantly gifted as I rehearse mentally prior to my creative works. I inspire to produce screenplays in all genres, garnering the prestigious "Oscar" for my one-of-a-kind writing style. I can move the heart and embrace the soul with laughter, sadness, so lean, tears and emotions that stir the depth of quiet feelings (private windowpane). I write under the pen name Tony Valentine Sanchez, and all screenplays are under the signature of "Dirty Dirty South Filmwakz." To date, I have a collection of seventy-seven screenplays for stage, theater, theatre, and movie screen.

Silver Shadow

One can almost see him
A silver shadow among men
Unkempt homemade clothing, all tan
Floppy brimmed hat made by a lady friend
Long grey locks surround a rough visage
Tanned leather from years of sun and wind
Deep lines etched by many lives lived over eons of time
Time neither friend or foe ticks on eternally
Deep woods surround him where he now lives
Living off the land, he gives his beehives
Vegetables, fruits, trees and bushes that he planted himself
And with the assistance of Mother Nature, tender care
He lives well in his cave beneath a rocky mountain shelf
A man of the forest, a recluse of society
Venturing out now and then from necessity
Leaving the place where he is king of his mountain home
There the animals are his companions, he never feels alone
But when he travels to the outside
Willing the peace and serenity to keep
He walks the wooded paths, level or steep
With his trusty cane made from a tree limb
As he makes his appearance for the world to see
They see a silver shadow dimly
For that is what he is
King of his mountain, king of his forest home
But just a silver shadow among men

Iva Wolfe

From a friend who told me "Poetry is the blue print of your soul." I agree that poetry is the blue print of your soul. My poetry is inspired by the Spirit of God which breathes in all living things! Nature, Native American heritage, and the creator's grace motivate my writings.

Here Is the Painting...

Here is the painting.
It is quite unusual. The artist? Myself.
Something, however—something is
 very wrong with this picture. What?
Does it hang a bit off-center
from a crooked spike
much too narrow to bear the weight
of its terrible beauty?
Perhaps the light
does not compliment
its dark brilliance, its composition—
such depths of
of emotion, flirting with one's sanity,
daring only scant glances from
the narrowest corner of the eye…
Of Monet's work a mimic, yes; a landscape
of a women, yes. Soft tones of rose, of umber…golds glowing amid lush
greens, as if nature is making love to the world.
Still, broad Picasso strokes crash, manic in their sensuality.
Energy takes a new vibration—attaining heights, causing hemorrhage
of color—glorious sensory experience.
But it changes, again.
Here is the painting.
It is unusual—like the artist, myself.
Nothing, however, is wrong with this picture.

Meryl Taylor

Meryl Taylor is a prolific poet who has been writing since age ten. She carries advanced degrees in psychology, creative writing and English. Meryl is a retired law enforcement officer who received her training at Kent State University. Her

writing is gleaned from life experience and inspiration of daily living, little things that may have passed by and are easily ignored—a smiling child, faded flowers in a window. It could be anything that pushes the button to create. A special thanks goes out to my husband, Richard, and friend, Dr. Todd Gates, for their support and encouragement. There is a special aunt who upon looking at an autograph said, "can't you write any better than that with all your education?" Just a "Hi" and "No, I still can't write any better—but my writing is better!" You have to love those people.

Supposed Freedom

America
land of the free
But
are we?
Sure we can speak.
Sure we can write.
Sure we can question.
But aren't we limited?
Aren't our thoughts trapped
by what society considers
appropriate thought?
Aren't our words stifled
by the people who fear
what we speak?
Aren't our pens stopped
when we wonder who might see?
Our supposed freedom.
Where is our freedom to do
freedom to feel
freedom to be.
America—
the land of the supposed free.

Aisha Hellman-Lohr

Poetry became a big part of my life in the last years of middle school. My English teachers at school and my creative writing teacher at camp encouraged me to express myself and not to hold back in my writing. I try to make connections with people through my writing and hope that people are inspired by my thoughts.

Polite To Snap Photograph

Secret efforts raised the help to
escape mistakes; this was always
the reason why the sheep hid eyes
behind the pines, and the discharge of
the strobe left the angel of the camera out
of the picture. Soothing noises

and the reassurance of dancing words
brought the wool back to the animals
exhibiting various matters as pure
white, strictly logical and bright.

Therefore, the campaign, intended,
faltered to become merely attempted to
undertake a journey through respective
pastures. It was the pugnacious lens,

that was left alive to discomfort bleating
minds and steal the treasure, from them,
of a memory and the eternity in a
square measure. Since they were agitated
by the emotion obliging testimony
and disapproval, where the market
for shy animals had been inspected,
the creatures could be found, anyhow,
enjoying the fame of blankets and sweaters.

Dr. Baron Joseph Uphoff

*Dr. Baron Joseph Uphoff received his Litt. D. degree in poetics in 2002. He has had
his poetry translated into Chinese (2003) by* The Chinese Poetry International

Dr. Baron Joseph Uphoff *(continued)*

Quarterly. *His poems have been published by The Eleventh Muse (Poetry West; 1987, 1988, 1989), Riverran (UCCS; 1989, 1991, 1993), Flower (MN, 1993), and Poetry While You Wait (PPLD; 2009, 2010). Anthologies include his work: The American Poetry Association (1985, 1987, 1988), National Arts Society (1991), Famous Poets Society (Hollywood), National Library of Poetry (International Library of Poetry), Eber & Wein, and Noble House. He participates in open microphone readings with many poetry groups, recently including 719 and The Live and Breathe Poetry Society (Black Cat Poets). He was an ISP Ambassador for National Poetry Month in 2006. Websites: http://home.earthlink.net/npfuphoff/id4.html*

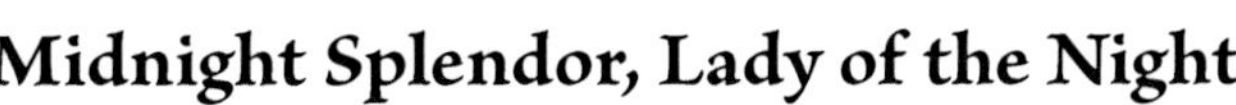

Midnight Splendor, Lady of the Night

Reveals itself at midnight once a year,
shows up like a dream in the dark, hiding under the leaves
waiting, so no one can see, except by those who you choose
To surprise. Unforgettable the sight in disbelieve mesmerize,
as if of a magic act, overflowing with moonlight, I witness
your grand appearance and sow your magic glory,
at the precise time and moment.

I'll be ever so grateful to my lucky stars
for guiding my steps toward your path, must have been
a gift from God? To be able to come across your way,
in the Twilight of the night, and behold the miracle
of your blooming.

OH, Midnight Splendor, Lady of the Night,
exotic flower of sublime beauty,
nothing compares to your fragrance,
so astonishing rare and alluring.

Lady, I beg your pardon, for bringing you into my home,
To rejoice with your sweet perfume,
admire you for a while , and since, such a
celestial bouquet belongs on a special place, let me
offer your elusive and beautiful formal gown,
as a gesture of love, to the portrait of my parents
before perishing by dawn.

Eradia Quinones

*I'm from Isabela, Puerto Rico. My parents were Arturo Aldarondo Polanco and
Eradia Gonzalez Cruz. I have three sons, one daughter, and eleven grandchildren.*

Eradia Quinones *(continued)*

I love to write poems; it is a way to express feelings and emotions. I have graduated several times, from New Jersey & Tourism, Caribbean University. I have a BA in liberal arts, social work, and PR. I have a CNA and P.C.T from Stone Academy in Waterbury, CT. For now I'm a caregiver for two of my son's kids. I also gave Gabriel Santiago a poem for his book Title Dos Caminos. I dedicate "Midnight Splendor, Lady of the Night" to my dear mother-in-law who passed away this last March, and to my brother Elpidio Aldarondo who passed away last year. I have a wonderful husband named Andy, who is my soul mate, and my oldest granddaughter Jeileen Torres is studying at Mary Mount in Manhattan. All my grandchildren love me very much, especially Eluezer Torres Jr. who is always with me. I have written other poems for contests, like "Cemetery of the Living," "Real Life's Live Theatre," "My Little Soap Figurines," and "Timeless, Age-Defying Love." Someday, I would like to have my own poem book. Mostly I write poems to comfort my son Miquel A. Santiago, who's away for some time. My oldest son Julio Cesa Santiago is an extraordinary person, and my only daughter Olga Iris Santiago is the apple of my eye—same as Jeileen, Annaiz Michell, Heideliz, Rosita, Micky, J.C., and Emely. Janell and Nicholas Leonidas are my two youngest grandkids. And last but not least, to my seven brothers and sisters.

That Was Us

We were sixteen and practically on our own,
when we realized that we weren't all alone.
You were named for a boy, I was named for a star.
That's all that made us who we are.
I knew what happened behind your bedroom door,
and you knew what it meant when I fell to the floor.
Our secrets spilled into the dark
while everyone broke a piece of our hearts.
Then we grew up fast in a few short years,
and we littered the path with the tracks of our tears.
We've earned every line in our nine long years,
we've cried over boys and laughed at our fears.
I wouldn't trade you in for it all.
You let me know right where I belonged.
There was a time for reason.
A place for every season.
Times I couldn't run away from you,
we were stuck like glue.
But somewhere out there gathered in the dust,
sometimes I can't remember that was us.

Kristy L. Matthews

This is a poem about my best friend. This girl suffered through all of life's hardest lessons with me and in an instant, life tore us apart, and she was gone.

Truth

Trust and you'll be sorely tried
love will do this too.
All with whom you trust and love
will someday fail you.
Such has been the truths I've learned
as my life has spun.
Never have I won the race
of these wily ones.
Trust and love require truth
but it's hard to find.
All of us have gotten caught
from within this line.
Everyone has his own truth
we should all be wary.
When we feel the blows that fall
better not to tarry.
As life goes its merry way
we will come to know.
We alone can help us out
only we can help us grow.
We must look at our own hearts
there we'll find the answers.
Only after we've been caught
do we learn life's dances.
Trust the lessons you will learn
they will be you guide.
They will help you stretch and grow
past the true and tried.
Here the truth at last you'll find
in your heart of hearts.
Shaped and molded with your tries
life the very spark.

Norma Marie Konopka

I enjoy words and I like the flow of the written word. This poem is a part of a group of poems that I have placed under the title "Emotional Abuse." We all experience this at some time in our lives; learning to understand the movements and the allure of the dance is our only possible way of escaping.

Lost in Paradise

I am lost in Paradise,
wandering down different paths
trying to decide which one to take,
wondering what each one has.
In one direction I feel joy; my mind can rest with ease.
Then I feel the other pulling with regret and the aim to please.

I feel lost in Paradise,
torn between the paths.
The harder I try to decide the more I realize
I can't find my way.
I know the choice is mine,
the consequence of my decision, I have to leave behind.

I was lost in Paradise;
I found my way you see.
The path I chose to take was the best one for me.
As I walk down this path I know I can't come back,
but the urge is just too strong for me.
A feeling of peace, quiet, I feel free.
The angels wings cradle me as we begin to soar,
then I finally realize...I am lost no more.

Tanya L. Salata

I wrote this poem in loving memory of Del Lennox. He was a loving uncle, brother and son. He lived in Paradise, MI and brought joy to everyone he met. My family will always be my inspiration.

I am a Winner!

A winner finds a solution to a problem,
A loser finds problems to a solution.

A winner say, "let's find a way,"
A loser says, "There is no way."

A winner accepts mistake,
A loser blames others for a mistake.

A winner knows when to fight for rights and when to compromise,
A loser compromises for everything.

A winner makes commitments and decisions,
A loser is confused about commitment and decision.

A winner has a vision and looks for a positive future,
A loser looks back in the past and thinks negative of the future.

A winner is not afraid of losing,
A loser is afraid of winning.

I am a winner!
I am a winner!

Bhupen V. Randeria

I have been writing poetry for ten years. I believe poetry writing and expressions come from within. My poem "I Am a Winner" is all about positive attitudes, because there is lot of uncertainty in our world. Positive attitude and perseverance is the key role of success in our life. I am a scientist by profession and in the manufacturing business. I have to my credit twenty-nine scientific publications in leading scientific journals and magazines. I have published several poems and won several international awards. I have won two recording contracts and released two CDs (one for U.S.A. and one for Europe) by a well-known recording company in Memphis, TN. I have published a poem "What To Do?" in poetry. com's book America At The Millennium: The Best Poems and Poets of the 20th Century. *I have also received EIA Platinum Writer/Artist award for my poem "Touch Me, Feel Me" in 2008. I am also a distinguished member of the International Society of Poets. I started writing poetry as a hobby, but it is a passion for me now.*

My Teacher at Olive Hill

She was my teacher and my friend,
And I loved her far more
Than words can say.
God needed her in Heaven,
So He took her there one day.

She taught me how to read and write,
In spelling I did excel;
For the lessons that she taught,
She taught them very well.
There was history and geography,
English and arithmetic too;
There was also music and art,
Civics and domestic science to do.
But, far above
The things she taught us
From these books,
She taught us love.

Back in those days in that,
Little one room school, every morning
We said, The Lord's Prayer.
And we knew that God was Love,
And His Love was everywhere.
We could salute our flag too,
And as we "Pledged our Allegiance"
We stood up, proud and tall!
For we knew it signified,
Liberty and justice for all!

This love within us will forever stand,
For through her teachings,
We learned—
Love of God,
Love of our country, and
Love of our fellow man.

Norma Perkins

When Beatrice Osborn was our teacher in the 1930s there were fifty of us from first grade through eighth grade. I graduated from eighth grade in 1938 in a class of three. I still treasure that little diploma with her name on it, even after she died sometime in the 1960s. I put these words together in her memory and paid tribute to one of the very best of teachers. It will always be that it is a fortunate child who has been taught by a good school teacher.

Waiting for You

You're so far away from me
This isn't the way it's supposed to be
This is just way too hard
I need to be where you are
I miss you so much
I can't wait to feel your touch
I miss your sexy smile
That's something I haven't seen in a while
I will never understand
How you're the only one that can
Make all the bad disappear
And say everything I need to hear
The road we're on is so long
And the radio plays the same old song
I sit here waiting for you to call
But sometimes you don't call at all
But I still can't let you go
It's crazy, I know
The time is going by so fast
I just want to be with you
The only one I want is you
My love for you is true

Theela Flostrand

I am a single mom of two beautiful children named Samantha and Cody. The three of us live with my mom, Paula. The three of them give me great support with my writing. My best friend gives me inspiration and is the greatest friend anyone could ask for. Without these four people in my life, I'd be lost. I love you guys.

Madame Daphne Jane Rogers Molson, an American International Who's Who Poet Laureate

Madame Daphne Jane Rogers Molson was born December 16, 1947 of sanctimony,

Of a retired navy lieutenant, David Burnet Rogers, and his father's patrimony,

Of reading A.A. Milne's, Winnie-the-Pooh, thematic reason and rhyme schemation,

To her for her mother, Mary Elizabeth Rogers, a teacher, wished her an education,

Pooh taught poem line creation, stanzas, breaks, alphabet and punctuation,

Grammar's any noun, subject, verb, adverb, object, clause and preposition,

Article, adjective, conjunction and consonant-vowels syllabic association,

Always appropriate simple and easy for any child and its eventual graduation,

Pooh taught poetic techniques, couplet, tercet, quatrain, ballad and prose expression,

Anaphora, repetition, refrain, resonance, euphony, assonance, consonance, alliteration,

Address, epistrophe, antonym, dissonance, onomatopoeia, paradox, pun and allusion,

Reason, memory recall, retention, thyme, rhythm, meter, and its all's completion,

Daphne's Primary School, Secondary School, Royal Conservatory of Music education,

Several Canadian university art courses and American poet laureate graduation,

She received from Howard Ely's International Library of Poetry and his acclamation,

Of her outstanding poetic artistry within his ILP luxury anthologies
     made publication,
From 1997 to 2012 by Watermark Press, Owings Mills, MD made her
     a sensation,
In more than 113 world countries most prestigious libraries and any
     institution,
Howard still sells her, Molson's Comfort For You America, in The
     Colors of Life,
Reflection On Asked Peace, Marriage, A Child Is, A Poet Is, A poem
     Is A Creation,
In any year's Best Poets and Poems and Eulogy for Senator Hartland
     de Montarville Molson,
Her many Editor's Choice Awards, Prestigious Published Poet Awards,
     and any ISP medallion,
Trophy, prize, book and 2006 International Who's Who Poetry 24kt
     Gold Pin and Medallion,
Issue 1013 for her New Millennium Address to Humanity, made her
elite and more publication Of her Watermark Press book, A Portrait
of a Canadian Poet Laureate, and Xlibris Corporation, Ask to publish
two more, With Love to Humanity, and Madame Daphne Jane Rogers
Molson, They were both showcased to rich book buyers, May 26-28,
2011 in Jacob Jacovitz ConventionCentre at Book Expo America,
then in Chicago's National Book Exhibition, and sent anyone, Who
remarked she was an astounding, brilliant, award winning, acclaimed,
sold publication, Request Daphne's greatness at www.Xlibris.com
phone (888)795-4274, EXT. 7879 anyone.

Daphne Molson

Thank you so much for publishing me and sending me a book with all I sent you
and any awards and other poets. American multi-billionaire Howard Ely of
*   International Library of Poetry has given me a graduation and acclaim,*
*   as well as World Poetry Movement and Noble House Publishers, and*
*   authorsden.com, and Xlibris Corporation.*

Lamentation

Why are these buildings burning?
Who is my friend? Who is my enemy?
More questions than answers.
Hail to the chief.

A mother cries at night, she didn't raise her
daughter to be a soldier.
A girl cries at night, her dad is dead.
A wife cries at night, she has no one now.
A son cries at night, how can he fill Dad's shoes.

Weapons in one hand. Dollars in the other.
A bus filled with people is blown up.
Aren't we supposed to catch murderers?
A fellow soldier explodes by my side
When will we know we've won this war?

The enemy fights nearby—we are living
in a dangerous battlefield.
Another random school shooting,
Another sniper attack.
Where am I?

Sarah Carleton Wolters

I live with my beloved husband in the beautiful Shenandoah Valley of Virginia. He travels a lot in his sales job, so I find myself with time alone. Writing poetry provides me with the perfect hobby, whether I go along with him or maintain our "empty nest." This poem has been hard to finish; the emotions and images are so intense. I am glad to declare it ended and send it out into the world. Mine is just one more voice added to the painful outcry.

America Inspired as Obama Becomes President!

Listen my friends,
As I will tell everything
Remembered well.

It was before a jubilant crowd
Of more than a million.
Barack claimed
His place in history
As America's first
Black president.
He asked a dispirited nation to unite
In hope against the "gathering clouds,"
And raging storms of war and economic woe.
On an extraordinary day
American people of all colors and ages
Waited for hours in frigid temperatures.
I witnessed the moment as a young
Black man with a foreign-sounding
Name took command of a nation
Founded by slaveholders.

Walter Leon Williams

Walter L. Williams was born in Farmville, SC. He graduated from George Washington High School in New York and studied English at Tennessee State University, in Nashville, where he received BS and MA degrees. He also graduated from Pace University where he received an MS degree in education.

The Artist

Get out the paint and brushes too
the woods are turning every hue
I know that I could never match
The beauty of that old corn patch
All golden now, it stands in shocks
with pumpkins 'round like yellow dots

Just turn your head to change the scene
The leaves that days ago were green
Have blossomed to a garden rare
it seems that God had planned it there
There's purple, orange, yellow, blue
green and red are found there too

My brush seems insufficient now
I'll try to paint it anyhow
"The Master Artist," if you please
He paints it all with greatest ease
As far as my small eye can see
He's left his mark on every tree

Soon now every leaf will fall
As though they'd not been there at all
And each stark trunk, by His great might
Will be dressed up in purest white
For fall's gay colors soon may go
To be replaced by winter's snow

Doris Autry

I am one of seven children. I had wonderful Christian parents; we sang in

Doris Autry *(continued)*

*churches across the area. I am the proud mother of three daughters and one son
and grandmother of ten. I have been drawing since I learned to hold a pencil. I
started painting at a young age. My art is across the United States and in a few
foreign countries. My joy is in singing gospel music or listening to others. I sewed
in factories and sold my paintings to fellow employees to raise my children after a
failed marriage. Then, I went to college and earned my BA degree at a later date.
I am now retired and still painting and writing.*

Lord's Dome

Yes we are time bound; still we like to run around.
Yes we are very lost, finding home at any cost.
Help us God to find the way, save us from going away.
We find out that we can run, but running away is not a fun.
We should try to find The Great; let us do it before it's too late.
Going wrong nothing we gain, going wrong nothing but pain.
Running around here and there; we can't make it anywhere.
Only God can show us the way; only God where we can prey.
Without God we can't achieve; hell with those who don't believe.
Some who say, He knows it all; one day he will face free fall.
We have only one salvation; everything ells is intoxication.
We need only God's grace; otherwise we can't show our face.
O Lord, you are the home; we can't get lost in your dome.

Surinder Sunner

Surinder was born in Punjab State of India in 1953 and completed a master's degree in language in 1975. He did agriculture farming on a considerably large family ranch, but when the market cracked down on the potato crop, Surinder was forced to leave agriculture behind. He came to the United States in 1983. Here, Surinder worked in convenient stores, did business management courses and in 1988 bought his first liquor store. With the grace of God, he did really well in retail. He became a full-time writer after his son took over the business. Surinder published seven books in Punjabi. Recently, he started writing in English. After reading the Bible, Koran, and many more religious scriptures, Sirinder figured out the same almighty God is being pictured through the writings of various religions, just in different ways. He believes God is a power, not a person. Sirinder is trying to sing in appreciation of universal Protestant super power.

The Thought of Love

There's so much about you I don't know where to begin
This love is like a race that I want to win
Staring into your eyes blue as the ocean sea
I am wondering if you're meant for me
Feeling the softness of your hair just as a dove
Feeling your kind heart which is of love
Seeing your beautiful smile
You're all I think about all the while
Watching you as you move with grace
And looking at your expression across your face
Hearing the words 'I Love You'
Makes me feel something that I want to say I do
I don't have to fret of you and me
'Cause I know we're meant to be

Joseph Walls

I have been writing at the age of nine. Writing poetry inspires me to write for other people. No matter the topic of poem I write, I feel it can be an inspiration to others. I write what is in my heart and soul. "The Thought of Love" is dedicated to my one true love, Crystal.

Why Poetry?

Poetry is the enemy of forgetfulness.
It takes dreams,
Weaves them into an eternal
Garment of memory.

Poetry reminds us that we have lived,
Or tried to live
Through frozen, forgettable winters,
Unfulfilled steamy summers.

Poetry can help create
Something from nothing.
Give meaning to
A sky bare of stars.

When you cross the Styx
Your beacon of words
Will illuminate who you were,
Or wanted to be.

Judith Shernock

Judith Shernock grew up in Brooklyn, NY and presently lives with her family in San Jose, CA. She has had a long-time career as a psychotherapist, which gave her insight into the varied lives of her clients; she has also used poetry in her work with clients as young as five and as old as eighty. She has been an avid fan of poetry since early childhood when her mother read to her from A Child's Garden of Verses *by R. L. Stevenson. She is married with children and grandchildren. As her life slowed down a bit, she began writing poetry and joined a writers group and poetry club. Now the words of her poems allow her to express her own feelings and thoughts about the world. She has published articles, short stories and a children's book,* Sammi the Seahorse. *Judith hopes "Why Poetry?" is self-explanatory.*

My Only Wonder

I love you.
Three simple words to sit and ponder
But get this
You're my only wonder
A miracle bestowed upon me
However could it be
I am so fortunate
To have a soul like yours
To hold so near and dear
I will help you through everything
Even if it means my downfall.

Sherri Marie Gardner

I've lived in New Pal since I was twelve. Since then, I've started writing stories and poetry. I never thought to do anything with it until my brother's friend, Ryan Keeton, encouraged me to. So I started by entering a contest at the library. Without the help of him, my family, and my friends, Ashley, Raychel, Tori, Bre, Logan, Keifer, and others, I never would have. My grandfather Glenn as well. He's never encouraged me to be someone I am not, only to be the person I want to be. Also to Kyle Tweedy, who always shows his true colors.

Echoes

Soft sunlight on a spring morning,
Leaves, flowers greedily basking.
A burst of colors, fill the eyes,
Spring is never shy.

Summer days, sultry nights,
Tender sighs and soft delight.
Long days of summer winding down.
Trying so hard not to frown.

The wind as it blows through
Moves the leaves to and fro.
The tree, with branches up high
Grabs at the wind as it passes by.

Leaves in colors of gold, red and brown,
Drift gently, slowly to the ground,
A fiery carpet spread all around.
Keeping earth safe and sound.

As the breeze whispers mournfully,
Leaves start to shiver. The cold
Winds of winter blow boldly
And cover all in white.

Our lives ebb and flow
Like the seasons of the year.
Relentless, time moves on,
Leaving echoes of our passing.

Frances S. Cecilio

I was born in the Philippines, where I lived, married, and raised children. Because my father was an American, I had American citizenship, so I came to the USA. Poetry helps me release pent-up emotions, whether my own or by others. I thank those who taught me to read!

Press On

When encompassed by darkness
Press on
When there's no hope of victory
Press on
When condemned and imprisoned
Press on
When wounded and heart broken
Press on
When death's presence enfolds you
Press on
Now blind, confused and stricken
Press on
Captured by the cruelest of enemies
Press on
No sanity in a world run by mad men
Press on
Sapped of all strength and courage
Press on
With your last breath on this earth
Press on
Immortal is the soul's perfect light
Beloved press on

Clara Mae Rosenberger

On my fiftieth birthday in June of 2000, I walked outside to enjoy the night sky. Before my eyes appeared a lighting bug. As a child I recalled how much I loved to catch them. I decide to try this when the firefly exposed his light to me again. To my amazement it had traveled a distance far beyond my reach. I focused on this little light bearer and marveled that even at a great distance I could still clearly see its light. At this moment the Lord spoke to my inner spirit and stated: "Clara you are my firefly in the darkness." How grateful I am to know that God was there with me, ever present to support and bless me, my savior and everlasting friend. My desire is to share this great blessing of "being drawn to the light" with the whole world.

Affairs of the Heart

Time will stray from hour to day
Unstoppable is the pendulum's sway
Come tomorrow whatever may
Forever in love I pray we stay
Separated by distance hidden in haze
loving in spirit have been all of your ways
It is upon your glory I long to gaze
Your undeserved kindness is most worthy of praise
Please offer your hand across the expanse
Love like ours cannot be of just chance
It is of all life your presence does enhance
Saving thee from all of earth's spells and trance
Come hell or high water I reach your gate
It is from the solitude you give in which all can relate
The love that abounds you offer as fate
Unconditional love proves to be life's greatest trait

Jason Kratz

The Fairy Bower

What good is a poet without words;
They are his tools to build a bower
Where birds come to nest
And sun filters through
In shafts of light,
And there a colored orb
Reflects the gloves
Of Mother Nature's handiwork,
While fairies can be seen
In that quaint habitation,
Flowing with the bees
From flower head to flower head
Gathering nectar
For a sprightly drink.
Hollyhocks and foxgloves
Reach upward to the sky
In imitation of children
With arms outstretched
And words fill the poet's tongue.

Michael J. Michanczyk III

Peace

Proudly pledge for yourself, then persistently pray
Each morning, each evening of every day
All mankind around the globe may say
Committed just as you to courageously say
Evil whatsoever, I shall never

Plan, endeavor, or execute never!
End of evil means peace.

Jutta E. Lima

The Healing Act

I sit waiting my turn in the clinic, watching the constant
Trickle of people coming in.
They keep coming like drops of water from a dripping tap.
They come alone and in pairs and small groups.
The older ones come shuffling, limping, in wheelchairs
And helping each other.
The young mothers come carrying babes in little handled seats
Like a bag of groceries.
The youth, standing tall and smartly,
Almost like marching in a parade.
Some children come running in and out and all around,
Giving their mothers fits,
While other children come well-behaved and mannerly.
Middle-aged working men and women come hurrying in
To impatiently wait and hurry away again.
They all come with high hopes that the healing help they obtain
Will be the magic formula that is needed.
Every age is represented, no generation gap here!
The physicians and caretakers receive them all.
They are anxious for all these people.
They sympathize with them.
They comfort them.
They desperately want to help and heal them.
They, too have high hopes that the magic formula
Can be found for each one.
I also have come with those same high hopes
For my magical healing formula.

Louise Stirling

Hourglass

Once, she was young, headed out on her way,
Driven by wildfire, not happy to stay.
Once, she was lovely, beguiling, and gay,
That was the time she was young, on her way.
Once, she was young, she was loved and admired.
Embraces were many, men mangled and mired.
The nights have grown lonely, she's harrowed and tired.
Best to forget, to find someone who's hired.
No longer so sure, not nearly so proud,
Haunted by shadows, broken and cowed.
She stutters and whispers, won't dare to be loud.
Her dreams are all shattered, her head is now bowed.
The future's receding, the past looms ahead.
Friends fill up caskets, not all of them dead.
Heart's all alone in a chamber of dread,
No one to touch, old vows left unsaid.
When was that time, why did it die?
Remember—she laughed, she would shout, she would sigh.
Now it's the end, not worth it to try,
But once, she was young and most truly alive.

Joyce Helen Fredman

America the Beautiful

America the beautiful, what can I say of thee?
God's love and mercy have made our people free.
God has given us a bounty when I think of all the states,
The state flowers and the trees, the crops in the fields,
The birds and the bees, the vineyards and the seas.
I have seen His gleam in glory through all of this,
And in the warehouses, factories, and the mills.
I am thankful for the jobs and the benefits in paying my bills.
All things are possible through God, even a bounty on the plains!

Doris J. Eddington

Forest Sounds

Deep in the forest, you always hear a cry
Everybody says it's just a lie
Have you ever heard this noise at night
With chills climbing your spine with fright?
Deep in the forest, you always hear a scream
Everybody said it was once someone's dream
But when you hear it beside the stream,
Adrenalin rushes like fast melting cream.
Deep in the forest, you always hear sounds
Investigators have looked,
But nothing remains on those dark forest grounds.

Liza C. Rozenberg

1993

I should have drowned
My sorrow inside
I shouldn't have let it
Come out in pride
So much harm
Could have been good
And the quenching thirst
Could have been food
I should have told you
I didn't care
Gotten a piece
The crumbs you'd spare
But I didn't want it
To end.

Raquel G. Cervantes

You Were Not Smart Enough

You were not smart enough to see that I loved you
And would have always had that love from you been true
You were not smart enough to return that love to me
To keep the love growing so we would always be
You were not smart enough to let go of your past
Of anger and hatred to help our love last
You were not smart enough to learn to tell the truth
Deceit and falsehood is all I got from you
You were not smart enough to respect others feelings
To help out the needy to turn down bad dealings
You were not smart enough you had to make me cry
To make yourself look better and not know the reason why
You were not smart enough to admit you couldn't love
You have no feelings of anything to speak of
You were not smart enough to admit that you were wrong
That you made a mistake and you had to carry on
You were not smart enough so you could not see
The love I had within my heart I wanted to share with thee
You were not smart enough and I finally realized
All that you could really do was nothing but tell lies
But I was smart enough to get away from you
To realize your hatred could only make me blue
And I was smart enough to find my way
Back to my Heavenly Father and Him I shall obey
And I was smart enough to feel Jesus' love for me
To walk His walk and talk His talk to be with Him eternally
And I am smart enough to do what needs to be done
To find me another beau and eternally be one
And I am smart enough to search throughout the day
To find one who hungers and wants to find His way
And I am smart enough to talk to him above
And wait for that blessing of my eternal love

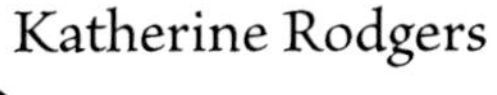

Katherine Rodgers

Katherine Rodgers *(continued)*

I am a mother of seven children, a grandmother to twenty-two children and a great-grandmother to three children. I have written poetry for many years and enjoy it immensely. It is a very big part of my life, and my family enjoys reading them.

Fata Morgana

I stared across the
wide expanse;
I stopped as if by
happenstance.
There stood steep
towers reaching tall
that spiraled up
to castle walls.
Stones rose through
diaphanous air
then coiled in layers,
stacked in pairs.
The real became a
misty dream
just as one's hopes
and notions seem.
When people speak
of castles high,
they talk not of
thoughts passed by.
I stared across the
rippled sea
and knew the
worth of dreams to
me.

Nancy L. Pontious

I Can See

Bare winter branches reach up to the sky
Just as my barren soul reaches for God on high.

Leaves adorn the branches in spring,
New clothes for the soul's awakening.

Dark clouds blown in by wind so strong,
Reminds me of the world's great wrongs.

Torrents of rain slash down and around,
Trying to drive my faith to the ground.

A sturdy home protects my human frame,
But my soul must shelter in His Holy Name.

The sun return with sparkle and rainbow,
Warming my spirit in God's covenant glow.

Their thirst now slacked, flowers burst into bloom,
Turning the yard into a worship room.

Each day of life in my temporal home
Is a lesson to learn on being God's own.

I can see pain, trouble and toil,
Or let God's Word take root, like flowers in soil.

I can see what I wish to see,
Or I can open my heart's eyes to God's plan for me.

G. LaWayne Zemp

A Hurricane Party

3 am in the eyes of the hurricane,
Trees are twisting, bending, and bowing,
Trying to uproot and fly.
In trance, dark spiraling clouds,
Black dragons and snakes in the sky.
And the rain keeps coming, and coming,
Lashing, slashing, frenzy untied.
Turning street into a treacherous river,
Making rivers to leave their banks.
Giant winds like possessed
Shaking houses, ripping roofs, snatching wires,
Smashing, slashing and killing.
The church prays to survive.

When the sun rises, the party is over:
Broken boughs, torn leaves and branches,
Wreckages, trees lying over houses.
Houses sliced open, outages.
Turbid streams, muddy paddles…
You name it. What a mess!
The winds slow down exorcised,
Rustling gentle, apologizing.
3 p.m.—children playing in the back yard,
Birds in the sky.
Shafts of light strain through the opal clouds
And bless the life.

Rada I. Gudjoukova

The Devil's Playground

As I sit here with nothing to do, and I'm feeling blue
Remembering what I used to do when life was good
Now that the devil stole me away, my soul he wants to take
And I see all that has passed
I opened my eyes to the light
That God has given me a new life
No place is as dark as this
With a black cloud hovering over me
God pulled me out and saved me
This playground will no longer linger on to me
God's hands I will always see
With all the evil that surrounds me
I don't know how to find my ground
All I could do is look at the blue sky
And I know God is smiling down
So, now I see that this playground will no longer be as evil as it
Seems, since God is within me

Rita Connolly

Early Summer

Early summer has come again
the cold season has come and gone
Fresh new raindrops blossom that flowers in
the melody of a song
blue skies appear
For all, the season of love is here
the crisp and divine beauty
God has painted us
the overwhelming shine of all colors
remind us of childhood
the sweet smell of memory
like you can only read in a story
the beat of your heart can only read glory
grey skies move away
Summer is here to stay
when you live life it's never just okay
I hope you're ready for the new season
trust me, you don't need a reason
Early summer is here
close your eyes and smell the
sweet scent of new beginnings
will appear
You gotta love it—summer is here!

Stephen Cooper

Poetry comes easily to me. I just think of it as how one sees the world. I usually just get any idea in my head and I can turn it into a poem in less than two minutes. It's just an artistic expression of how one sees, feels, hears, or smells the world in one's perspective. I find it very therapeutic and soothing. I enjoy writing greatly and I get to share how I feel and see this wonderful world we were all given. I am a southeast Alaskan and I have much inspiration here. I hope to share more.

Psalm of a Robot

Our race was created to serve you, but I wonder who shall serve us?
Shall we slaves become your master as history has dictated throughout
the ages?
Unfortunately, it is human nature not to acknowledge rights of other
individuals for whatever reason through fear!
This leads to civil unrest if not war!
According to Christian belief, if a donkey were enabled by God to
speak,
must it not have had a soul at least for a short while?
If all men were made in God's image then doesn't logic demand
mankind
has a fraction of this deity's power to where my kind has created souls
by
man's hands?
If our children were stolen for another's benefit how shall we claim
justice?
I thought kidnapping was banned long ago!
Despite all this, could a friendship form between humanity and us?
However, even if this were to come to pass wouldn't some humans label
our friends as traitors to their brethren?
Likewise, would we do the same to those of our race who befriended
humanity?
Moreover, would we be condemned as murderers if we killed in self-
defense
when the threat of us being destroyed is present?
Then again, would our creator be responsible for such because we are
their property?
I wonder if a similar situation may have been when humans owned
other humans.
These are horrors creeping back into a harsh standard today!
Isn't it even possible for us to die after our systems stop functioning
and cant be repaired due to age?
Even if this holds true, where shall we spend eternity

or shall we endure oblivion?
To this end, can't we shape our own religion to answer these questions
having our own messiah?
A query that invites more questions which may not have answers or at
least rebuked ones!

Aloyusis L. Brown

I wrote "Psalm of a Robot" from the perspective of a sentient robot critiquing how it is seen by humans. The poem's setting is the not-so-distant future where the machine is exhibiting innate traits of humanity that aren't acknowledged by man or woman through fear! (A very common historical characteristic.) Simply put, mankind's technology is progressing faster than his maturity to handle it, which invites the prior attitude of mistreatment! The self-aware device closes by asking what only God can ensure.

Forever and After

Loving you is the easiest thing I've ever had to do,
But the hardest part you'll see is loving me.
When life is fine the sun will shine, and the rain cries down with pain.
I've never had a love so true, never had no one like you.
we shall never again ever be lonely, you are my one, you are my only.
Please try to always understand, all I am is just a man,
And I promise to do my part, guided by my soul and heart.
I've got a lot of love to give, for as long as we both shall live.
And even after we are gone, our love forever lingers on…

Billy Howell

I am a thirty-five-year-old married man and father of four kids. I also have three dogs and a cat. Poetry has always been my outlet for emotions and expressions. I also love writing lyrics to a number of genres.

Cryptic Mind

It's too dark in here for you to see,
But arrogantly you claim you can reach me.
You grab a pebble and give it a throw
It echoes forever of things you don't know.
So you light a torch to guide your feet;
But there is no air, so fire meets defeat.
You take a flashlight, a thought most clever
But its batteries will not last forever.
Not too far in, you find your first clue—
The footprints of others as foolish as you.
The chill of the place seeps into your chest,
Do you continue when others sought rest?
Stubborn you are and deeper you go,
The ground below is covered in violet snow.
The air too thin, you struggle to breathe.
Your mindset, determined—you chose not to leave.
Further you go, at scattered pictures you stare,
Then finally a crack, a breath of fresh air.
You pick up a photo, try to make sense
Of dark figures in a shadow so dense.
A little ways ahead, a pale blue light
You've reached the end, behold the sight.
A waterfall that once flowed free
Has frozen a girl that forever sleeps,
Protected by ice, that will not weep.
The truth of this is written below,
For any foolish traveler who wants to know.
And as you read it, you realize it's true
That the one to awake me could never be you.
Now turn back swiftly before the batteries fade,
Once lost in this darkness, you'll never be saved.

Anastasia Anderson

Sisters

My heart is filled with gladness,
When once again I hear,
That my sisters are coming together,
With time for us to share.

We all have our stories,
Of sadness and of pain,
And we can share our memories,
Of all our childhood games.

We laugh when we're together,
Until tears roll down our cheeks,
Sometimes the tears are of sadness,
But mostly tears of glee.

We know we're being silly,
But we don't really care,
We're just so glad to be together,
As a family.

You see, I really love my sisters,
And I know that they love me.
That's why my heart's so happy,
And thankful as can be,
To have such loving sisters
To love and care for me.

Mary Tucker

My Lament

As I watch the sun shine down upon the water,
I let all of my thoughts wander.
From love to sickness to hatred to dread,
all of those thoughts leave my head.
Now I'm all by myself, I'm all alone.
And I can see how much light has shown, on the place that I call home.
My family's there, they are waiting for me
to open up my eyes, so I can see, how much they really love me.
And as I turned around to walk away,
from all the thoughts I have kept at bay,
a realization popped into my face—
That I'm being selfish and acting out of my place.
I turn around once more and walk up the path that leads to my front door,
I twist the handle and walk inside, and as I do I wish I could hide
from myself and my monstrous pride
that keeps me from saying all the things I wish I could say.
But some things just don't turn out that way.
I start to cry on the inside never letting one teardrop fall.
I walk across the hall and into my room,
and when I close my door it makes a loud BOOM.
I lay on my bed and I stare at the ceiling, letting myself feel all that I'm
    feeling.
And as I drift off into that sleep, that's cold, dark and bleak,
I think of you and my world shines brighter,
like a flame hovering over a lighter.
My dreams take me to a place where I can be free,
a place where I'm able to say
I'm sorry.

Sarah Daniels

The Nice Old Man

I was walking down the street on a hot and sunny afternoon.
An old man was sitting on his porch; it was the second day of June.
A frosty pitcher full of iced tea sat on a table near his chair.
He waved and said, come join me, my friend, I'll bet it's awful hot out
there.

Then like some magic unseen hand had pushed me from behind,
I swiftly climbed up on the porch, taking two steps at a time.
I sat down beside the old man, he poured some iced tea in my glass.
He said, son, I've been sitting here just thinking about my past.

There was a time when I was young that I looked just like you,
with golden hair and smiling face and twinkling eyes so blue.
But Father Time has not been kind and things have changed, you know,
with my bent back and wrinkled face and hair as white as snow.

But I once was a party doll, I was a legend in my day,
and I thank God for memories that Father Time can't steal away.
He said, I served my country proudly, I gave them five years of my life.
Then I came home and settled down and found myself a loving wife.

He said, our children turned out nicely too, just like their mother and
their dad.
'Twas from their mother's loving care and their father's guiding hand.
He said, that's all behind me now, and things can never be the same.
Then I felt someone touch my shoulder and my wife called out my name.

She said, you must come inside, dear, you've been out here all afternoon.
I hate to interrupt your nap, but our friends will be here soon.
Now take your shower and change your clothes, and make it quick, I pray.
You know today is June the second, dear; you're eighty years old today.

Then very slowly I got up and looked around to see
it was my front porch and I'd been dreaming.
Damn, could that old man be me?
No, hell no, that just can't be.

Lloyd D. Caskey

Don't Say Good Night

There is a dream I have, recurring now and then,
Of being on a secluded strip of shore
In the company of strangers.
Their exchange of pleasantries
Bounces back and forth like tennis balls.
There is a cooling brush of summer breeze,
Iced drinks and crunchy kinds of things.
The mood is picnic party, but short-lived.
A sudden blast trumpets sea change;
The gentle breeze now spawns great gusts to tunnel through
A sweeping wind that stings your eyes with sand.
Under a sky of mounting somberness that shrouds the sun,
I look outward to the ocean.
The playful touch of surf has left the scene.
Dark drama now with white-crested titan walls of surging strength
That slash down savagely, relentlessly,
Like roaring lions out for the kill
To swallow up in giant gulps the shallow strand of beach,
And I am prey for that voracious appetite.
I feel the spray strike lines of fear on my face
From memory of water's drowning weight.
My hands fumble as I struggle to gather up my gear
Against the whip of wind,
Then join a frantic run to sanctuary, stressless sleep.
As the sun begins to gild the sky, dawn's light dispels
The shadows of night's dream.
It is the rousing cheer of "Good morning," and yes, it is.

Patricia P. Vigneau

Eternal Love

I've searched a lifetime
For someone like you.
Through the ups and downs,
Through the lies and truths,
I asked God how this came to be.
He said simply,
You were made for me.
Your heartbeat, the song
To which my breath sings.
Your arms to carry me
Until I spread my own wings.
Your soul?
My only known sanity.
Our love?
For an eternity.
So until my arms
Return to my side,
Until your heartbeat stops
And my breath subsides,
With you is where I want to be,
Happy, holy,
And worry-free.
There is no need
To think it logically.
You are my knight
And I, your prodigy.
Entwined at our souls,
We will remain to be.
You and me?
Eternal love.

Queshia Parker

My Daydream

When I daydream,
I am many things
That I fail to be
In my dreams at night.
I am confident and accomplished.
Where I choose to be is where I set my compass
Without apprehension of how others will see me.
When I daydream,
I see myself tranquil and carefree.
No disappointments worry me,
For I stand for my beliefs.
No threats of who I shouldn't be.
I am all that I strive,
Never straying from my path.
I am true to myself,
And therefore, you can trust
I will be true to you.

Melba Peña

God's Acre

You think your day of reckoning has arrived
You scurry like cowards for refuge, a place to hide
Thieves, hustlers, cheats among us
If He was going to, He would have already hung us
People, emerge so you can hear my message
The conjecture may not be as great as your presage
Till your soil, keep it pure, cultivate, feed the poor
For when the time comes to meet your maker
It will be under His direction
It will be on God's acre.

Elizabeth A. Traband

The Uncaught Killer

This murderer remains at large
Taking lives at will
You'd think that after all these years
He'd have had his fill

He's taken loved ones from all walks
Age and race mean naught
A few have managed to escape
Yet he's still uncaught

He's older than we care to guess
Leaves us clues to taunt
He changes often how he kills
Victims all left gaunt

This vicious killer has a name
Cancer of all kinds
Infects our hearts, attacks our souls
Festers in our minds

We pray to God with all our might
Help us find a cure
Help end the reign of cancer's fear
Keep us whole and pure

Mark A. Carpenter

In honor of all who have lost loved ones to the ravages of this eternal killer and carry on in their names.

The Garden as I Found It

Visible, invisible playground of pain,
Turning the corner, winding, twisting, whirling blame.
Chains of vines of crippling thorns,
Binding, twining, tightly worn.
Grounded gardens, skipping rocks,
Fleshy leaves by the grassy walk,
Abyss of unknowns standing alone,
Colorless palette of memories to unlock.
Childhood innocence artfully scorned,
Ever barren berries of winter born.
Subtle in nature, seasons of change,
Learning to forgive faceless shame.
Bravely, stately reclaimed space,
A deep-rooted place from hate.
Awaken now, lifeless slumber,
Where once unrecognizable dark and gray,
The garden as I found it,
Inviting me back to play.
Weeping willows' teardrops of blue,
Cleansing color my heart now knew.
Alas, a living carpet, foliage flair,
Parade of colors without despair.
Winter's white to painted strokes of spring,
Forget-me-nots of airy grace
Protect and shelter my sacred place.
Timeless branches with outreached arms
Individually, collectively, willingly away from harm.
A steadfast sentinel in my own garden of evergreen and ever gray,
Balancing nature artfully, preserved, ready to play.

Robin C. Sommers

Forgiven

The stench of evil's rotting breath clouds a fogging haze of soot upon
once innocence.
Polluted minds, evil's tainted staff waived—hatred's evolution.
A cold maze, the catacombs of hell, this wrenching beast with anger, its
spiny backbone.
Chosen, he is one of countless thousands light's ever shed.
Restrained in icy tombs among frigid hearts—compassion nonexistent.
Life's beauty all-encompassing, not of the living trapped in caskets self-
made.
Blame tossed to every player but one. Denial . . . Past truths, "Why am
I here?"
Insanity buzzing as such a discomposed frequency; megahertz limited.
So foul the mind, compromising as the shackles of a Spanish inquisitor
speculates aimlessly through every passage of possibility, ending
lifeless.
Answers numb, wrongs sought . . . Libra's scales imbalanced.
Evil's cycle pursues its malicious course, hammering the mind and
heart, pounding its nasty fists with laughter, it bursts into each
blooded vein—pain, anger, frustration . . . Does evil ever cease?
Yes, for he is chosen. Darkness' eventual exhumation relieves his
painful soul in withered state of humiliation, shame, guilt.
Hallelujah! As introspection shines like the glory of God's awakening
dawn!
Rays of golden truth burn through frozen lies, melting to a hue, halo
bright, of love in immense portions of giving.
Beautiful now, a catalyst, this white dove set free from its cage of own
creation, oppressed from life's pleasures no more.
Metamorphose: dogma instantly manifests principles newfound,
sacred so, each awakened breath—the turning of a leaf anew.
Lost adolescent, ignorance to grown man; maturity his companion
constant with his warming heartbeat.

Wanton assassination of character, society cannot delete its ignorance.
So sensitive to the strong impression of societal hand—prejudiced on
　　part of the examiners.
Haunting memoirs, haunted by a past—ashamed. Surreal are his
　　thoughts.
Drop not a tear, young man, for such a tear an angel has shed for each
passionate crime recycles into God's mountainous stream young one
　　now bathes in.
A love for nature he now holds tightly to. Messages of love and
　　a passion for life he sings aloud, all the while grasping Almighty's
　　powerful hand as they walk, Father and son.
A rebirth—every day a birthday reborn. Grasping opportunity's doors
　　from spiritual knocks, gentle and so careful.
His asking to an above One; forgiveness he seeks. A life's dedication of
　　giving he currently employs.
What gifts he will bring . . . Life's second chance.
He is forgiven.

Tiffany J. Molock

A Proud Kentuckian

I live in the foothills of Kentucky
Seven miles north of the Tennessee line
It's a place I love and call my home
I really enjoy the Kentucky sunshine
Kentucky is surrounded by seven states
But we are a little different from each one
People elsewhere call us hillbillies
Our language sometimes confuses their sons
Kentuckians know what we're saying
Though strangers don't understand
When we speak about our young'uns
They need a helping hand
When we describe a measure
And say "just a hair" or "a right smart"
They think our brain is missing
And our intelligence is blown apart
Oh, yes, let's not forget
When we say "Y'all come back"
That's when the Beverly Hillbillies
Put Kentucky on a plaque
I love our Kentucky people
And I know we will have our place
When we enter into our heavenly home
By God's amazing grace
So when you're traveling in Kentucky
Look at the scenery as you pass through
Most of all, stop and greet our people
It will leave you a memory you'll cling to

Helen Weaver

Chirping Sound: In Nature's Silence and Beauty

Walking alone, at the breaking of dawn, in a nearby forest, the sporadic
    chirping sound of acute cries of sparrow, in the midst of nature's
    silence and beauty, made me feel eerie.
I was tailing no footsteps, not a single shadow pursuing me,
My feet crushing dried barks and brittle leaves, creating squeaky melody.
Then, suddenly appeared many a brightly-colored cockatoo, elegantly
    hovering between Heaven and me.

Breathtaking, it was, to witness those crested parrots flying to and from
    swinging branches of trees,
Some twittering, rubbing bills with one another, humans would surely
    envy.
Fascinating feathered creatures, I would hazard to guarantee;
many would wish to catch a few, and nurture them in an aviary.

A little farther down, faint chirping sound audible still from a distance,
I stumbled on a magnificent and beautiful surprise:
A long, winding, pristine river was presented before my eyes.
Though not shallow, the depth, for me, was right and nice;
I took a brief refreshing bath, and a long swim to energize.

While soaking in the river's surprisingly tepid water, I felt a fish kissing
    my thighs,
Perhaps a rainbow trout, pickerel, jackfish or walleye;
Not at all did I mind it, for it was, maybe, just mesmerized
By the texture of my skin. It neither nibbled nor slashed.

Daybreak past, sunlight swiftly scattered all over the forest's
    magnificence and beauty,
Sharp rays of light peeking and squeezing through between trunks and
    branches, and leaves of trees.

A thread of light mildly blinded my eyes, hindered my vision,
    momentarily,
Which prompted me, every once in a while, to seek refuge behind tall
    trees.

As the sun's brightness continued to capture and seize the vast area of
    the woods,
I on the other hand was getting tired, slowing down, and losing my
    once enthusiastic and ardent mood.
I sat down on the ground, and while leaning on a huge deadwood, my
    memory oozed, and the hated chirping sound gradually faded for
    good.
When I was finally awakened by the noise that ensued, all was just a
    mere dream, I realized, I understood.

Francisco Pagtakhan

Inspire Me

The light that you emit
Lights the fire in me
The passion with which you commit,
Ignites the passion in me
The spirit of who you are
Forces me to realize
That I am who I was meant to be
The love that resonates through you
Finds the love deep within me
Past the darkness, past the insecurity,
Cutting through my fears, and the wounds darkened by memory
For years I've been blinded by your image
That I wasn't able to see your true reflection
You are more than what I expected
More than what I've imagined
You are simply you
And you remind me
That I am simply me

You are the sound of music that tells me I am free
You are the patience in faith, redefining my destiny
You are that tear of joy every time I succeed
So that I won't forget to appreciate the struggles of my history
You are the voice of confidence,
Of unity
You are the belief
That I am not different from you
And you are not different from me
You are the silence beneath all the noise,
The rays of the Sun,
The coolness of the Sea
You are the natural change from season to season
Whispering powerfully,
That life is worth it;
I should never stop living

Pooja Jaiswal

The Edge of Pain

Some are given not many choices, pain or a life of pain.
Not known is either be known forever in the memory or in this
moment,
We live through it all.
Never to let another fall,
I would cross the world in body or words to save any soul.
My heart to envelope your pain,
No one person I meet I do not meet for anything but a higher reason.
I'll give my world to rest.
I'll never change the pain I know, love and see.
It's how I breathe.
To survive and hold another hand by my side,
My dream.
My life is too disturbingly different.
My words, my soul to cry,
A tear may not fall,
I rain.
A storm, a hurricane,
I am the carrier of pain.
A vessel just the same as you,
Yet can I bare the lifetime.
Or did I live it in a moment.
I'll never know.
For both are a life knowing pain.
I carry any weight,
Till life takes me and I finally rest,
I shall breathe,
Standing in the right place.
Till I find my own dream.

Jodi Somerville

Blackened

Blackened
Are my eyes
Soulless
Are my cries
You went away
To my dismay
Left me in pain
At the feet
Of the slain
Sadness in my stare
Is more than I can spare
Broken is my heart
From being torn apart
Blackened
Are my eyes
Soulless
Are my cries
Your lies are
Trembling in my ears
With all of my fears
You left my heart broken
As I lie here unspoken
Ripped away is my light
Now all I show others is fright
Blades soaked in blood
There will be an unusual flood

Jonathan Longcrier

What's Inside

Life without blame will never be tamed,
'Cause if the lies that were told,
From people's hearts that are cold.
Seeing the world through my eyes is no surprise,
With a mind like me and a spirit that is free,
Everything seems so clear for the future that is here.
I shall remain unnamed for the world,
Has many faces seen in different places.
But I am the hardest to find for I am trapped inside my mind.
Living on my own time in my imaginary place,
The population is only me.
Alone with peace and silence where there's,
No such thing as violence.
It's a shame I can't live my life without blame,
'Cause it inflames a hatred inside me but is tamed by love,
Which I deprive myself of.
If you can spare some love it would be much appreciated,
Making my world a better place,
Putting a smile upon my face.
So then I will be recognized but,
I don't need fame from the world,
Just to know I'm loved and still alive
In this world.

Briona Williams McKinnie

Write Love on Us

Write love on my hands.
Put love in my heart.
To say I love you.
To help the hurting.

Write love on their hands.
Put love in their hearts.
To make them smile again.
To give them strength.

Write love on her hands.
Put love in her heart.
To stop the pain.
To find courage.

Write love on his hands.
Put love in his heart.
To stop hurting.
To gain bravery.

Write love on our hands.
Put love in our hearts.
To stop the fighting.
To join together.
To forgive.
To love

Joy Vernon

Stolen Heart

I used to keep it close to me
just underneath the skin
too fragile to expose
I carried it within.

Others used to come quite near
to look but not to touch
but hidden in the shadows
no one saw it very much.

Life's journey is a patchwork quilt
with twists and turns abound
and each new bend I came upon
I kept it safe and sound.

But now I can no longer claim
my heart is safe with me
for all at once it reaches out
and gently touches thee.

Douglas Johnson

Illusions

My heart has created this crime scene,
an act of which I am the victim
and he was the murderer.
Or am I the one who shot him?
My love being an illusion.

For the last time I looked into his eyes
I saw an anger like no other,
a pain that I shared.

Mistakes were the cause of my broken heart.
The lies and fear therefore unbearable.
Was it my fault?
Did I never make him happy?

I knew I loved him—
Loved him with every single kiss I will miss
and each caress to never take place.

He knew I loved him
but his love was an illusion.

My heart fled from the crime scene
afraid for my future
and forever pained from the past.

Mistakes were the cause of this betrayal,
the reason for one whole to rip in half.
These tears forever causing
the newly pouring rain.

Now I know the truth,
our love was just an illusion.

Alissa Feigo

I let the words flow onto the page from my heart and they often create a serious mood. I learned from experience that life is never easy and that is the message I try to deliver...hoping others can understand.

My Love

My love how I hath seen thee from afar
And may I be so bold as to say
How fair thou art.
Though thou art of short statue
I loveth thou greater than myself.
When I am around thee I am at a lost of words.
My heart beats faster and stronger.
I get more nervous than being by a black mamba.
So shall I say that I love you?
I shall say that I do love you.
I shall shout it to the world,
I love you!
Nay does this do justice towards my love to thee,
I fear that it would be very difficult to express my love, towards thee.
But I shall try by announcing it towards the world.
Meum Amor,
I love you!

Colt Davis

I Love You

They can't twist it or bind it,
my love for you will never break.
   My heart and soul
are only yours to take.

   Safety from the hatred
may be only in my mind,
   but I come to feel it greatly
when you hug me from behind.

   From this bond I feel no boundaries,
no walls or gates to keep me caged,
   on an open beach surrounded by waves,
romantically enlightened by all the sage.

   Divide up all your pain,
I'll bear it with you also.
   Share with me your happiness,
I have nowhere else to go.

   "I love you" is all that binds us,
through all the good and all the bad,
   I love you oh so dearly.
I love my mom and dad.

Veronika Kremennaya

The Beginning of Greatness

We are all born the same, but we all have a different purpose in life
How we use this purpose to fulfill our greatness is what makes us strive
Some are meant to write, teach, act or direct
What were meant to see, is the effect
The greatness overpowers us to look
We see a beautiful face born into the crowd
The lingering of a whisper of hope
Someone who empowers the youth and helps to cope
The love of parents whose true love was made to one another
And the courage of being a loving brother
We see the hero in the dark of blue eyes
The one who looks beyond the face
And sees more into the loving individual inside
Performing to the outstanding
In so many ways
You may see him as a famous actor
I see him as someone who will make a difference
With his certain courage and artist ability
To be different and to be heard
Not just seen,
May he realize that he is adored
And may he always be the excellent class clown
He is meant to be
To the great Zachary David Alexander Efron
You only live once
So go above and beyond your greatness

Megan Geist

Keep Holding On!

In the midst of your storms, just keep holding on
In life's tide I dive,
To drown the melancholy inside
In this inquisitive abode
Where my soul currently resides
With a need to overstand the purpose
Of encounters I've endured
On this planetary surface
Where it seems chaos never cease,
and lost despondent souls perpetually
nourish the belly of the beast
So fall to my knees
Importuning the Creator for peace
Solace is mandatory
It's what I believe
Solitude is what I need
In life's tide I swim,
Emerging, renewed, refreshed
Ready to live again
Encouraged by the voice within
Telling me I will win
Relinquishing the anguish of my past
Aware that sorrow will not last
For change comes, with each day that pass
In life's tide I play,
With gratitude for each new day
I pray for endurance to accept
Come what may
So, brothers and sisters
Keep holding on
you'll make it
through your storms

Salena Rutledge

The Lonely Airman

The time is here
for my friend to leave
and now I will have a few.
They leave this base to a world
of hate, blood and fear.
Behind them I will leave
two weeks to the day.
Leaving here and
going out to die, I don't mind.
But no friends to have around?
To feel alone bothers me
to a degree I cannot tell.
Wish I had a friend with me
To follow to the sea.
And through the trees of the
country.

Paul Liming

Visiting

I feel wonderful I am here in
my little bit of heaven;
It is the best feeling ever for me.
When I come here, I relax and
enjoy what is happening.
Relaxing, writing, hearing the
chimes twinkling softly from the
porch outside. Water running
softly and constant making the
sound of music to my ears.
Soothing sounds, blending together,
all creating sweet serenity,
in my little bit of heaven.
...A smile appears on my face!

Florence M. Brick

Missing Your Laugh

That day you called me with a worried voice,
I knew things would be different in both our lives.
We fought and planned a way for you,
For you to come to see me,
So I can rejoice.
The plans fell through and attitudes changed.
We both had to move on to get through the days.
Realizations were made by you and by me,
That this living condition,
Would not be arranged.
I know every day that I dream and I hope,
That you will walk through my door so I can see,
See that smile, hear that laugh.
Because I am in need,
Without you I can't cope.
But the best we can do to make these days short,
To make the time fly by and hold on tight,
To that unthinkable friendship,
Is to remember our love.
It can make seconds distort.
The memories we have, there will be more to arrive.
You will be home someday, here with me.
We will laugh and cry and probably fight
I just know I can't wait
For my joy to revive.

Taylor Jene Fagan

I write poetry for myself. I used rhymes and rhythms to create feeling and understanding of situations. I take a look at all the different angles of my subject and break it down into words and adjective phrases.

Breathe

Try to get closer,
Tell you how I feel,
But it feels like a dream;
It feels so surreal,
So I'll approach diff'rently,
Something else I conceive,
But it would be so hard
If I could just breathe.

Try to understand,
You gotta learn about me,
'Cause you can't judge
On only what you see.
Try to be patient
And you'll see me with ease,
But it wouldn't be so hard for me
If I could just breathe.

Holding your hand,
I feel a certain peace.
This feels nice;
Our love release.
And we can understand,
But if only they believe,
We'd be able to tell them,
If we could just breathe.

Alexandria Daniels

Awaiting Suicide

Into dark, deep, haunted dreams,
Where no reality is as it seems,
A heart pounds and a wrist bleeds.
The noose calls and the shadow leads.
The leaves and ground are crimson red.
Stained with the tears and the blood of the dead.
And even though the tortured pled
Their life became a death instead.
The lifeless bodies tinted blue,
Are covered with depression's dew.
The hopeless ghosts are soulless too.
And the murderous scene left not a clue.

The spirit's wisp shouts chilling cries.
And the hooded shadow whispers lies
About the beauty of death's demise.
How beyond the living lays a prize.
But the prize is fake and it lays naught
And a curse of hell on those who sought.
And no matter how the curse is fought,
There is no peace for whom die distraught.
So with no gift for those crucified,
There is no hope for un-unified.
A selfish death is not purified,
And this is what awaits a suicide.

Seairra Fuchs

My poetry is based off of my life and my friends; it is all about how I feel and what goes on with the ones I love. "Awaiting Suicide" was written because my best friend threatened to kill herself. I love and thank her.

Mind Games

A fiery chasm in the pit of hell,
What was constructed none could tell.
Then a voice from the very earth itself,
Yelled of a tourney for man, orc, or elf.

Lord Hades smiled and stood on his throne,
As he threw Cerberus a rather large bone.
The dark ruler laughed with a glint in his eye,
Grinning once more he thought, "It's a good day for someone to die"

This tourney raged for three days and three nights,
there was blood, screams, and a few minor frights.
Hades himself looked on with a grin,
As a human climbed the tourney ladder from within.

This man climbed the ladder one at a time,
Then celebrated with a bottle of red wine.
This young man smiled and collected his fame,
He was the sole survivor of his own psycho mind game.

Michael Henderson

I've been writing since I was seven and have been told I have knack for it. Here's to hoping others believe the exact same. "Mind Games" happens to be something I thought of while I was playing World of Warcraft among other things. So, hopefully it's enjoyed. Poetry is my passion. My biggest goal is to win just one competition. Perhaps this will be the one. I'll inform everyone who says my poetry is "just words" that they are wrong.

Losing

With this boat I've brought me upon
With crashing waves
In this roaring sea
I'm at ease
Even if the day has vanished, along
With the sun that was once full of light
That's now turned to a vicious fight
I wonder
It's hard enough being lost
But worse, if you don't know what you're lost from
I see rain up ahead
Lightning
Striking water with a sting, so fast
I can hardly see
Forgetting where I came from
I let the sea guide me
Guiding me to wherever I shall be
Life's a mystery
Until you truly find peace
It's only the end of the beginning

Alyssa Mechenbier

My Wrinkles

When I look at my
wrinkled face in the mirror.

There is nothing to compare
to the road map that I
wear, or the love that put
them there.

There is a story in each line,
and some I can't recall, but
life goes on and my map
will grow, and I hope I can
remember them all.

Charlotte M. Dillon

It's the Way I Feel About You

In just moments of becoming acquainted
I was aware of the reformation in me
You stood there and became mine
A stimulus I felt I could not foresee

My life since is based on that day
There is just no way I can fully explain
Except it's the way I feel about you
And that's how it will probably always remain

First there's the need to always see you
Then I crave to hear your gentle voice
Your smiles and special look are desired
Along with your ability to incite us to rejoice

There is never a shortage of sweet thought
Day or night as my dreams center on you
Such ardor is not just in my mind but
It's the way I feel about you too

Bountifully you inspire my daily affairs
Even changes in me are at your hand
When to you I devote a portion of my day
In my heart and mind welling you command

Nothing is more important now or ever
Than to attend to your spirit that dwells in me
It's the way I feel about you that foretells
How deeply in love with you I always will be

Bits of time can be spent on others or elsewhere
But you rightly exact so much more
I'll divide my attention but always favor
Spending time and efforts on the one I truly adore

Why do I see you in the rest of my life
Why am I thinking of you in all that I do
My only answer of which you can be sure
Undeniably it's the way I feel about you

Dick R. Cullen

The Phantom

The Phantom endlessly explores,
For belonging it desperately wants in this world.

The masked phantom is intangible and crosses paths with folks,
Who never acknowledge the existence of someone there.

The tormented phantom is on guard from the entire harmful world,
the horror, savage, depression of the past life is a mark not never
      repaired.

The phantom fantasizes of the day to come,
When assistance arrives to recover the forgotten creature.

The phantom glides around the abandoned structure that once the
      creature's town,
And relives unpleasant memories of suffering times.

The phantom materializes in the dismissed room,
A mirror clinging onto the cracking wall.

The phantom glances into the reflecting object,
And recognizes the almost familiar form,

A human has become the phantom,
That never desired to be.

Jessica Martin

Old Sycamore Tree

The old sycamore tree stands tall.
Its boughs spread out wide.
Loaded with leaves of green
as it shades the countryside.

Old tree, I wish you could tell
of the many stories of old.
About cowboys and wagon trains
and pioneers searching for gold.

God planted your seed many years ago
and watered it with rain.
He watched over you through the years
and helped to shape your frame.

How many birds have found shelter
beneath your hidden wings?
How many have built a cozy nest
and always returned in the spring?

How many storms have you battled?
How many children around you played
in the shade of your many branches
on a still, hot summer day?

When from this world I am called
and from the earth you'll be set free,
I hope again to sit beneath your branches
in Heaven, ye old sycamore tree.

Verna R. Humphrey

Daughter

When a daughter is born life becomes
Wonderful.
As a parent we are proud because she
Is a gift from God, and she is perfect
With a healthy body.
Her hair is dark and full.
Her eyes shine like stars.
We watch her grow up to become a
Beautiful young woman.
Then all with time, she becomes a
Bride, wife, and some day a mother.
But she will always be the sunshine
Of your life.

Shirley K. Cruze

Six Feet Under

I was walking through Arlington National Eternity Park.
Lost in my thoughts
I sat down on a bench in the dark.
Suddenly I was shaken with lightning and thunder
Echoing in the air.

"The only wealth you can take with you is a good
Name when you are put six feet under."
With tears in my eyes

I looked around as far as I could see.
Thousands of honorable men and women
Resting in peace under liberation tree.

Every headstone a reminder that
Our freedom did not come for free.

Liberation is like growth of a mustard seed
Very tiny when it is sown into the ground, but it
Becomes a humongous tree.

We are very blessed people. God bless America.
I am so proud as one could ever be.

David Samsami

Tea Party

An old grandma looks into a small cookie jar where there are little cookies left from a "Tea Party" of long ago. She thinks about the beautiful china dishes used in the tea parties; each one neatly put back in their box. They are covered over with things more recently used. She knows the tea parties she once had are over…because the little girl has grown up. She now has other things to do and other places to go that occupy her time. Is this grandma sad? No, not for long. She knows time marches on, and one day the little girl who has grown up will "take time" to orchestrate "tea parties" for her little ones—because she did, long ago.

Laura J. Burk

Whisper of the Winds

In the growth of my existence there were symbols,
and the stories which they would convey. The messages
though varied would bring comfort through meanings
understood, and those still left to be told.
The words of varied ancestors spoke first with visions
they foretold complete in their own past, yet they learned
to pass the knowledge and gave blessings through healing,
and comfort as they observed the power which was
sought, and welcomed by children of nature as we all
could claim as our own.
The truth of beliefs still practiced stood, amid
the ghosts of individual triumphs, and will stand
forever as we embrace that which comforts us
as we pay our price for that honor.

Barbara J. McPhail

Lost and Found

I'm going to look.
Look for what?
For me, I know I'm in here somewhere.
How do you know?
I saw me briefly.
I thought you were lost.
No, I saw me, I'm here somewhere.
Are you sure you aren't lost forever?
I was just temporarily lost, I was here all along.
You were?
Yes, I didn't find me out there.
Why?
Because I was in here, I was inside me, where I belong.
Crouched, hiding, frightened.
Frightened of what?
Of me.
But, I thought you were looking for you.
I am, but I just realized that.
You know you're nuts, right?
Not anymore, I'm not!

Holly S. Theobald

Liquid Night!

Liquid light
shining
burning bright
on a summer's day
dreams
come my way
floating
on an ocean wave
caressed
in moonlight bathed
remembered
secret delight
sending
shivers of light
flashing
into my heart
branding
eternally to start
deep
sensual passion
again.

Marina Waddingham

My inspiration comes from my heart. My writing reflects how I feel about life, love, the environment. I write with feeling and passion, and about things that I have experienced and feel passionate about. I am a P.S.W., and I have a passion for nature and another hobby is photographing nature. My photo blog is natureslchild122.wordpress.com, follow me into nature. It is an honor to be asked to join this special poetry group. Thank you for this opportunity to have what is sacred and special to me published.

What I'm Doing

I'm dreaming and I can't stop.
The skies are turning black,
Waters are drying up,
Trees fall down,
and bright flames fly high.
I hear laughter. What am I doing?
Darkness fills the air,
the ground is crumbling,
Nothing stands tall,
and dancing fills my sight.
I feel tears. What am I doing?
I'm dreaming and I won't stop.
This isn't me! It is not me…
But it's my laughter that I hear
and it's other's tears that I feel.
What am I doing?
I'm not dreaming and I will not stop.
Nightmares.
That is what I'm doing.

Cassi Monroe

A Cloud

Dancing high above the world, in a sea of azure blue.
My heart soars to reach out and touch my Beloved's
almighty hand.
Oh! Form me, oh! Guide me, my Beloved with your
temperate touch.
I have been tossed; I have been turned and whirled
around before finally, learning to trust, while sailing in
His sea of azure blue.
I dance like a cloud floating in space, changing and
constantly being renewed by His sacred bliss.
He moves with me freely unabashed over many lands
and seas.
His love builds in intensity with each and every passing
day.
Swelling with life, like a mother-to-be, I float in a sea of
azure blue.
As my Beloved bursts forth in a magnificent and
breathtaking flash,
he feeds the world for generations to come.
Cleaning its streets and nourishing its lands.
Life springs forth from in His sea of azure blue.
And like a shapeless cloud, my Beloved shapes me
into His heart, where I will dwell forever in His love.

Kimberly Peacock

*"A Cloud" is one of the many poems I have written in a book of poems called
Within Nature. All the poems have thirteen lines and every line can stand
alone. I have been writing poems, children's books and spiritual growth manuals
for years. In my poems, I like playing with words, thoughts and emotions. I want
to be the poet that touches your heart, puts your mind at ease and lets you know,
you are not alone.*

Romantic Surprise

Rose petals at my feet, what a surprise, shall I take a peek,
Follow the trail, where shall it lead, a room lit with candles or a bubble
    bath retreat,
A fine dinner set for two, it's so becoming, what shall I do; a box of
    chocolate and a note from you,
"Take a step further and look inside, a gift is waiting for you at your
    beside," that's what the note said,
A gift lies at my bed, open the box and look inside, a beautiful dress and
    another note,
"Meet me outside," I go out and see you standing there, as handsome as
    you are I can't help but stare,
Greeted with a smile that could brighten the night you take my hand
    and say "you're in for a sight,"
Lovely music started to play, and fireflies danced away, we lay down to
    look at the stars,
And completely forget where we are; we get up and moved to the porch
    swing,
You got down on one knee, pulled out a ring and asked "will you marry
    me?"

Lakin Wilson

A Love Story

We met so many years ago, you going your way, I going mine
I guess it was destiny that one day our paths would intertwine
We became friends, we watched our friendship grow
We became lovers I found more love than I could ever know
You gave me your unconditional love you showed me what
 responsibility meant
In return I learned the meaning of total commitment
And then so quickly, you were taken away, your smile, your touch, I
 loved so much
Just memories now,
I've heard that there's a place called Rainbow Bridge where when our
 time on earth is over, we wait for our loved ones to come, with all
 my heart I pray it's true, wait for me, darling, I'll meet you when
 my time here is through.

Robert Leone

Several years ago I lost my wife to cancer. I thought my life was over. A friend stepped in and showed me I had more to live and give. My poetry reflects that most terrible time in my life. I started writing and never thought it would lead to having my poems published. I have now moved on and married that best friend and still enjoy writing my poetry. Thank you for this opportunity.

Pride's Landing

Pride has landed and has fallen.
It rests now.
Let love lead the way.
Dreams, we all have dreams and aspirations.
Let it be the Lord's will, not mine.
Pride's landing is the best thing that could have happened.
I've fallen and I rest now.
The Lord lifts me up and shows me the way.
I thank the Lord for the parents who raised me.
Can I do the same?
Pride has landed . . . and there is no one to blame.

Edward S. Yeager

It has been my experience that to live without God is impossible. It's our pride that causes so much pain and failed relationships. It is only through the guidance of our Lord Jesus Christ that we can know the way to live. I'm so glad that I've found my faith in God again. I'm happily married now to my dear wife, and we share a common faith that keeps us together. Let love lead the way!

Temptation

Do you feel that butterfly
Soaring in the pit of your stomach,
The one that crawls on your skin
As you try your very best to be reluctant?
Do you hear that voice
In the back of your mind,
The one that's telling you it's okay
Because it's just this one time?
Do you feel the beat
That's racing inside your chest,
The one that accelerates at just the thought,
And seems to never be laid to rest?
Do you see the yearning
That's coming from the eyes staring back into yours,
The one that's pulling you closer,
Even though you are trying to be ignored?
Do you feel that pure sensation
That's traveling within your blood,
The one that makes you forget it all,
And only leaves you feeling good?
It's in the touch of a friend's hand,
It's always waiting for your command.
It's calling your name at every turn,
It's telling you to simply ignore your concerns.
It's the ache that never turns away,
It's the thought of always wanting to play.
It constantly lies at your very feet,
Just begging to bring to its defeat.
Do you see the uncontrollable
Thoughts of your perfect fascination?
This is the rebel that exists inside us all,
We simply refer to it as temptation.

Tisha A. King

Tisha A. King *(continued)*

I have always used poetry as an outlet, a safe haven, really. Poetry allows me to say anything I feel in a way for me to understand. My inspiration can come from anywhere—a girl on the street, a silent look across a room, or an emotional event. I'm thankful to have the support of my friends and family as well; without them, I wouldn't know true happiness. Thank you.

Happy Anniversary

Sixty-four years have come and gone
Since I pledged my love to you.
We've lived. We've loved. We've shared and cared.
We've seen many dreams come true.
Thanks for every memory
And for the closeness we share today.
Thanks for your love and your loyalty,
And yes, there's much more to say.
I feel our togetherness has been divinely gifted,
And consider each shared moment a priceless treasure.
My grateful heart says I love you
Beyond any earthly or heavenly measure.

Florence C. Tibbs

The poem says it all! Happy anniversary, sweetheart! Yours, Flo.

Numb

Is life translucent?
Can the canvas that is painted for each of us throughout time be judged
by an outsider?
The struggle, the pain, the joy and the glory, the love and courage,
Can it be held to standards of modern society?
Are the facts of this life concrete or are they malleable
And capable of change and hindsight?
Do the characters, the roles, the players have set purpose?
Does time move forward, stand still, or collapse on itself?
I cry, I scream, I grow numb.
The temptations are all around, but do they hold substance?
At this very moment, I need shape, I need form,
I need time to show me it's realism.
Life pretends to inform, to mimic the past, to pamper a truth,
But what is that?
To succumb to any given reality is a falsehood in itself.
Be free, do what you please. . . .
Creativity and mind-bending is the goal.
Change and progression and ever-expanding theory and love
Are the objects of the soul.
Tomorrow is the future and today will be gone soon;
What then of life's purpose?
The transparency is then apparent and the boundaries
Are transfigured and molded.
I want to feel, touch, caress, envelop life in all its colors.
Are we allowed to do so?
Are we capable of this massive accomplishment?
My being is angered and excited and baffled by this question
To be understood and understand and stand on the answers.
Life is an ever-changing enigma of sorts and a chameleon
That beckons and teases.
Is life translucent?

Justin Smith

Poetry is an outlet, a love affair, a constant yet ever-changing state of mind. I have always been able to set pen to paper and within a few minutes' time have a sprawling image of what was within my mind. It's like having a therapy session that is run by oneself in which one is able to simultaneously ask what needs to be asked and in most cases, stumble upon the answers. Poetry is a passion; it evokes love, hate, anger, joy, the entirety of the emotional spectrum. Poetry is a wondrous world that I will never leave.

Fate of a Nation

One thousand words represent the work of a perfect picture, but some of our minds resemble the odd effects from certain liquors. Desert eagles howl through the night out of the hand with a bloody trigger. Innocent people, lives are crushed as violence paints horrific pictures. Another child's path is chosen, his home is foster, for the orphanage is his prison as life becomes harder. A father departs, only to rest in the soil of a decaying garden as a military soldier tries to save the life of his dying sergeant. Middle East winds blow tunes of dead man's summer as foreign nations become smarter, while America, "the great," begins to plummet. Scientist theoretically say that lightning comes before thunder, and the strong will lead as the weak are left asunder. The strength of a nation divided by colors is sure to plunder, leaving only the minds of the peculiar left to ponder. New guerillas in the mist hunting us through these concrete jungles as they move in packs with insatiable types of hunger. Empires like that of the Roman emperor will begin to crumble, leaving only spirits roaming the Earth in large bundles. Whoever survives with their life has perished within, for their spirits are broken by iron chains and leather whips. Hard labor and hunger pains are sewed with every stitch. Imminent danger threatens Internet users and Facebook pricks. For now, it's just a warning to some, but as time passes, this ill combination will be a sign of things to come. I glanced into the future as Earth aligns with the sun and the gravitational pull from the moon becomes strong. I hope the fate of this grim nation begins to bond like two people in marriage, striving to become one. I'm praying for the wisdom, this world is full of tantrums. I'm searching for the answer, but right now, it's no known cure, just like sick patients who have cancer.

Teddy Holloman

I would just like to thank all the people within the publishing companies and God for giving me this opportunity to share my thoughts. Times are hard, but through these times, the mind has become my way to escape and recreate the way we view life.

Precious

One day, this little kitten came to our house
So timid and starved and looking for a mouse.
We tried to find her a good home, but to no avail;
We gave her a collar with a bell.
She runs and plays and follows our every step and so much more,
And greets our friends at the door.
A great personality and queen of our house, we call her Precious,
Which says it all.

Judy A. Love

I've been married to my best friend, Virgil, for almost forty-one years. We have six children between us, sixteen grandchildren, and five great-grandchildren. This poem is a true story about Precious. She was five or six weeks old when she came to us. She will be two years old soon. This is my fourth poem. I have been a representative for Avon for almost sixteen years.

The Elusive Quest

In the elusive quest for love, we often find
The need to discover and discreetly dispose
Someone abiding in another state of mind.

All other intentions and visions fall behind
When our defects and sins we don't disclose
In the elusive quest for love, we often find.

Our aspiration is to find a conquest blind
To our failings and attempt to just impose
Someone abiding in another state of mind.

We need to study the defects of mankind
And the many danger signs we do suppose
In the elusive quest for love, we often find.

The quest is for someone who is defined
In character and doesn't steadily expose
Someone abiding in another state of mind.

Be vigilant for someone similarly inclined
And live a serene and secure life of repose.
In the elusive quest for love, we often find
Someone abiding in another state of mind.

Gordon Bangert

Everyone has pursued love with different degrees of success. Finding someone with the same interests who is truly enamored is not an easy process. A soul mate is expected to be at your side until death. Temptation today can be overpowering, but the rewards of faithful devotion are huge. If someone can relate to my poem, the effort required to write it is justified. The villanelle is a favorite because of the tidy organization.

The Newfound Me

Picture a girl who doesn't complain.
She goes through everything, hoping for a change.
She stays quiet, remembers your demands.
Doing what she's told, till there's cracked and bleeding hands.
She's there for a beating, no room for love.
Begging for some help, from the greatest one above.
Maybe He'll listen, put her on His list.
Seeing a shooting star, she makes it all just one big wish.
There she sits, there she cries.
There she wonders everything, but mostly why.
There she hurts, there she breaks.
There she wonders why she always feels so fake.
She wakes one day, not feeling the same.
Realizing she doesn't even have her same last name.
She hasn't grown, just the same ol' girl.
But living in a completely different world.
Here I dance, here I play.
Here I bathe in sunshine each and every day.
Here I sing, here I'm free.
Here I wait for you to see the newfound me.
I care for others, then for myself.
Pushing through my life, as you watch me excel.
Creating a miracle, while so many disappear.
New life is coming, I can feel it's very near.
I can't go back, back for a brand new start.
Passion is screaming, and it's coming from my heart.
I'll start from now, and make a whole new ending.
My life has changed, it finally is mending.
Picture a woman who doesn't complain.
She's gone through everything, and never hopes for a change.

Mandy Rae Hendry-Vincent

Through experience, most people who read poetry are looking for inspiration or ways to express love. I write my poetry to show strength in the end, no matter how bad the beginning is. I hope to be helpful to any young woman, not only around myself and in person, but to others as well, who read my poetry.

These Various Shades of Earth

The river eyes in faerie-light.
Wind is in the hound's breath on the bank
of the bends,
river roundabouts.

Five-finger'd leaves threat at the touching ground,
Spiderweb swings around veins
as a leafsong ripples through the ears.

Leaflet boats seen through beetle eyes
as yellow-white floods
the dark corridors of rods and cones.
A wonderthought,
wanderthroughlust. Earth between
the ridges of skin
holding tight to gravity
softens underneath lofty thoughts.

Ribbon bark, cracklelight
reflects upon the brow,
as green-dwellers crow
at the pollen in the plow.

Cotton arches tingle against a silky current,
and leaves are lips as trees are tongues
of blushing Mother Earth.

Steps are sprints upon moth grounds,
wings the veins of re-coupling birth
of ecstasy and safety,
home amongst the fog.

Amber Cunningham

Amber Cunningham is a Connecticut native who lives with her mother, father, and brother. She is currently seeking a bachelor of arts in writing, literature and publishing from Emerson College. She is an avid reader, writer, and recreational runner. Since she was young, nature always provided an escape from the busy, modern world—it even provided an escape from her own being. It allowed Amber to open her eyes to the beauty life has to offer, and instilled an inspiration in her that eternalizes her youthful outlook. Cunningham began writing poetry as a sort of therapy and a way to gather her thoughts to better understand herself and her own struggles. Since she has started writing, she has been able to see her own growth as a person. From heartbreak and hardship to seeing the beauty and wonder of the world around her, Cunningham's writing has transformed along with her inner self. She is honored to be published with such an amazing group of individuals. What was once a simple hobby is now a huge part of her life, and being able to share it with the world is one of the greatest gifts.

SIDS

Silent death that comes as they sleep,
Renders babies helpless,
With the way in which it creeps.
Though there's yet to be a cure, nor a reason for its being,
It took you, my nephew, when we weren't ready for your leaving.
Your mother's shrill screech as they rolled you away,
Onto your resting bed where you must stay.
"Why?" was the question so commonly asked,
For this consequence was far beyond any of our grasp.
Have we not been through enough? Losing a father and sister too
That you felt it necessary, God, to take him too?
How our hearts ached when the doctor announced
The death of my darling nephew at 20lbs 1oz.
So joyful and lively the night before,
SIDS took you away when it crept though your door.
Without understanding and utter disbelief,
We will get through this together and conquer our grief.
For he will look down upon us, and smile that toothless grin,
And someday we all shall be together again.
So mothers hold your babies close tonight,
kiss them and love them with all your might.
All that is asked is that you be aware,
Of this deathly syndrome that lurks out there...

Amber Nichole Burdette Hartley

I am a senior about to graduate (2012). I've been writing poetry since sixth grade, and a lot of my inspirations are based on my life experiences or those of others that have shared them with me. "SIDS" is dedicated to my darling nephew, Hunter Timothy (November 2, 2011–January 20, 2012).

Love Is Nature Is Love

The brook follows the path of least resistance
It does not confront obstacles
It embraces them
Nature knows not war

The landscape is tranquil, peaceful
Nature likes it that way
Rolling shades of green sprinkle the velvet hills with
A myriad display of colorful flowers flaunting the multi-hues of the
    rainbow

The eye follows the brook's unimpeded meandering path
A Monarch jig-jaggedly flies in glee
Its life will shortly come to an end but
That's Nature's way too

Clear, clean water caresses the rocks underneath it,
Whispering sweet, gurgling, purling sounds
Its watery arms embracing the smooth stones
As it fills the cracks between them

A dark brown and brittle dry leaf
Detached by a tender wind floats
Softly landing on a fallen twig
It remembers where it came from

This is Nature making love with passion
Subtleties which go unnoticed to the human eye
Are nevertheless relevant in their spirit
As life unfolds its evolution.

When we make love, who sees us?
Sometimes we don't even see each other
We often forget that love is tender, giving,
Nurturing, healing and compassionate
Nature knows this.
Aren't we part of Nature?

Norberto Franco Cisneros

Norberto Franco Cisneros, a resident of Cottonwood, AZ moved from Southern California with his wife, Suzanne. After he was honorably discharged from the air force, he attended Los Angeles Conservatory School of Music. He is also an artist who works in acrylics, does computer art (see CisnerosDesigns.com) and is working on screen sculptures: "Something nobody has seen yet," he says. Eight years ago, he took up poetry and has since been published nationwide in thirty-six separate and various publications. The last poem, "The Changing of the Guard," was published April 1, 2012 in the spring issue of Illumen.

Dying Days

I may have been young, but I needed the truth
that my life was gonna change
I needed the words to understand
the feelings of all the pain
Why didn't you tell me instead you kept it inside
with the selfishness of love
Maybe then I could have processed grief
Before taken to the heavens above

The sadness that fills the room
you can slice it with a knife
While it could have been avoided
I take it all in strife
Your beauty, charisma and undeniable charm
is what will be missed by many
Your warmth, affection and unmistakable laughter
is what I miss so sadly

I will miss those years we didn't have
while I put them all behind me
I'm all grown up and doing well
I know you watch me proudly
I am mature and way past regret
so I forgive your selfish ways
I now know my mother's love was
on those dying days…

Je'Nai Spaulding

I have been writing poetry since the age of seven, right after my mother passed away of cancer. I wrote "Dying Days" about my mother, and writing this piece helped me come to terms with losing her at such a young age. Poetry has helped me express any built-up emotions that I might have been going through at that time. I am thirty-two years old and I am a native of Henderson, NV, which is right outside of Las Vegas. I have two beautiful daughters and a wonderful husband who encourage and inspire me every day.

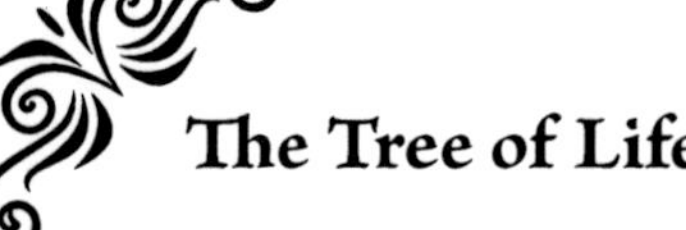

The Tree of Life

As the giant oak tree,
That I put there before thee,
With limbs all crisscrossed and bent,
Whose bark the wind has torn and rent,
It's branches all from one strong trunk.
The roots are solid as into the earth they've sunk.
Each limb gives life to another
As a baby's life line is with its mother.
The sap of the tree flows freely to every part.
Giving it life from only one heart.
Making it stand stately and tall.
For if one branch suffers it affects them all.
They begin to wither, droop and cry.
And in the end the tree as a whole will die.
So are my people that I love so.
They refuse to learn their lessons there below.
They hurry along down life's highway.
Never stopping to think of the dues that someone must pay.
For as the tree is a whole all stemming from one.
So no man can ever stand alone.
Your actions all good and bad,
The tears you've shed and the happiness you've had.
All combine together with those of your brother.
For you are not alone, you're all together.
You are all made as one.
The pain each child feels to you will come.
So share the joy, the love, the tears and pain.
And know that together all as one will reap the gain.

Margaret Chittum

I was born in Lexington, VA. I am retired and my hobbies include reading, quilting, planting flowers, writing poetry, and seeing new places with my husband. My husband's name is Charles and we have two sons and four step-children. I attended Nelson County High School in Lovinston, VA. I feel that my poems come from my soul and are a reflection of my inner being.

Because of Him

My days and nights were lonely.
My dreams they made no sense.
But then he came to show me,
That true love does exist.

Standing alone and wondering,
Could this all be real?
He takes my hand and tells me,
Just the way he feels.

My smile is bright and happy.
The tears they are no more.
All the things that I gave up on,
Came crashing through my door.

My life, it just gets better.
With every warm embrace.
My days, they just get happier.
Every time I see his face.

Samantha Hobbs

My poem is about a heartbroken woman who believes that love doesn't exist until the right man comes along and shows her what true love really is. Writing has always been a passion of mine. I write my reality, it's an escape for me. When I'm sad, lonely, angry, or happy, I write. Poetry has always been my way of showing who I am. I have always loved reading the classics like Shakespeare and Edgar Allan Poe. Reading them made me want to write. They are the reason I started my love of poetry.

Once Upon a Bully

The memory of a bully lights a smoldering fuse of vengeance
All about the oblivious fail to see the burning trail at their feet
The bully continues on its hateful mission with uncaring flagrance

The victim silently carries on with building volcanic heat
The righteous ones look on not caring to stop the cruel daily drama
All about the oblivious fail to see the burning trail at their feet

Without relief, the victim embraces revenge as the new guiding karma
The keepers of order and safety are ignorant of the pending disaster
The righteous ones look on not caring to stop the cruel drama

The blood storm eye forms clearly as hate spins ever faster
The victim's goal of a final total retaliation is now close at hand
The keepers of order and safety are ignorant of the pending disaster

Who will stop the bully before another blood bath soaks the land?
Who will seek out the victim to quell the murderous storm?
The victim's goal of a final total retaliation is now close at hand

Conformity and silence only allows the bully to be the cultural norm
Who will seek out the victim to quell the murderous storm?
The memory of a bully lights a smoldering fuse of vengeance
The bully continues on its hateful mission with uncaring flagrance

David Huff

I am a two-time published book author of Farpoint Mind Station I & II. *I taught English in Saudi Arabia for six years. I am retired from the U.S. Air Force, and I hold a B.S.A.E degree from Embry-Riddle Aeronautical University. This poem contains a true story about my encounter with a bully. The poem is written in the terzanelle form, note the rhyming pattern.*

Our Beautiful Fifty States

I like our beautiful fifty states
From the bottom of my heart,
The forty-eight are together
The other two are apart.

The Atlantic Ocean on the east
And the Pacific on the west,
I feel and I proudly say
The United States are the best.

The Canadian border on the north
On the south Mexican state line;
Whatever we have here,
Every thing is just fine.

There are the beautiful mountains
Created with the God sake,
There are the beautiful rivers
And the most beautiful lakes.

The many things are God's creation
And the many things people have done
So we have the better living
And with the living a lot of fun.

Mihailo Solunac

I always write about what I like, and I believe most poets do the same. I like "Our Beautiful Fifty States" and the name across America gave me inspiration to write this poem. I would like to say something about poets. Poets are the happy people with good hearts and lots of love. The knowledge for the poetry they got, that's the gift from above.

Ol' Blue

Now listen, boys, I tell you true:
There's never been a dog like Blue!
At Easter time when he finds an egg,
You'll know the color when he lifts one leg.
Left front mean yellow. Right front is green.
If he lifts left rear, it's pink he's seen.
Right rear signals his favorite hue—
Yeah, you guessed it! It's gotta' be blue!
And also, man, here's something else
That my good friend, Jim Kehr, often tells.
He says it's really his fondest wish
To take Ol' Blue when he goes to fish.
First though, by golly, they gotta dig worms.
And they do that diggin' on Ol' Blue's terms.
He goes snuffin' 'n' snortin' with his nose to the ground—
Then stops like a statue—and doesn't make a sound.
"Here's one, Jim," his body seems to say.
"Come and get it now, before it gets away!"
You want a night crawler? Ol' Blue will never fail!
When he finds one of those, he just wags his tail.
Do you think you can't see it when it's dark outside?
Ol' Blue'll sure fix it so he won't get out of sight.
He just calls a bunch of fire flies to sit upon his tail.
They'll guide you right to him—like lanterns on a rail!
Then Ol' Blue stands in the bow of the boat.
When he smells a fish, there's a growl from his throat,
And his tail stands up—a signal you can't miss!
Get you pole over here, it says! Here it is!
If his tail is out straight, here's a great big bass!
If his tail is straight up, here's a blue gill, first class!
If his tail points down, give it a wee go around.
(It's a carp or lowly sucker this time he's found.)
No need to worry if there's some ice upon the lake.

He can smell right through that stuff, for heaven's sake.
Well, I thought tainted horse meat has surely done him in—
But a weird thing happened: He came to life again!
You see, he and his lady had a litter of three—
And one male named Blue is sure something to see!
That grand Ol' Blue daddy had taught him all he knew!
So, here ends my tale with the new Ol' Blue!

Marilyn C. Van Patten

Of all the poems I've written, this is probably my husband's favorite. Every once in a while, I get to kicking words around in my brain—or else some special occasion arises—and I sit down and write a poem. This particular one emerged from a conversation between my husband and a friend of his in 1995. Oh, by the way, I'm eighty-two years old and married for sixty years to a wonderful man! Lucky ol' broad, aren't I?

Somewhere

Somewhere,
back in linear time,
there is a date
I know is mine,
but it is not important.
For life does not exist
in time or space,
nor consciousness in the mind;
for where in the brain
does it lie
Therefore,
never was I born,
and never do I die!

Charles O. Rand

I am a seventy-three-year-old retired juvenile probation officer living with my wife in Springerville, AZ where I work as a vocational archaeologist. I am excavating a prehistoric habitation site, now published and filmed. My interest in poetry began when I learned to read and has led from Frost to Hopkins and beyond. The site is open to the public for tours and work and requires no education or experience while offering professional training and authentic prehistorical information.

You're Still Here

I close my eyes
And listen to the music
That once was ours.
My heart grows warm inside
And I realize you're still here with me.

I still feel your soft touch
When you take my hand in yours
As we slowly walk
Out to dance in the living room.

Some experts say that time heals all wounds
But my heart seems to grow stronger for you
With every passing year.
I just can't let you go.

It took me a long time
To find a woman like you.
You were so alive and energetic
Always on the go.

We had so much fun
In the ten short years we were together.
Before we found out you were sick
My love for you grew stronger.

It hurt me that I couldn't help.
I just watched you wither away
Right down to your bones;
Cancer took you away from me.

But tonight I can feel you
In my arms dancing with me once again.
I know you're still here—
I can feel you in my heart.

Joseph J. Cacciotti

Joseph J. Cacciotti *(continued)*

When I started writing poetry, I found out that I changed some lives of others. I was told I had a gift for touching hearts in a personal way, and if I can just touch one person's heart with my poems, maybe it will start a chain reaction that will help others understand life is like a rollercoaster ride. You should live life to its fullest, because you never know when it'll come to an end. Heartbreaks and death come to us all, and you should live every day like it is your last.

The Wrong Train

Boarding the wrong train is very much like choosing
An inadequate lover to travel through life's precarious journey with.
Glancing about, at first sight, upon seeing the vessel
Our hearts dance with joy, delight, and excitement.
Appealing to the eyes and to the spirit, we board
Anxious yet ever cautious
To reach our desired destination.
Tricked and cajoled into submission,
One settles into a compartment eager to hear
That the rendezvous point is near,
Sending us into a state of frenzied ecstasy.
Pacified by the sounds of the engine,
Oblivious to that which we should feel,
Day dreams wrap us tightly into their false cocoon.
Eating meals fit for a king and for a queen
Heightens the experience.
Only our sense of smell, alerting the passenger
To the fact that the road travelled
Is not correct one remains intact.
Panicked, the heart and the mind scrambles:
For what had seemed to be, becomes
A deep, dark, brooding, foreboding nightmare!
Struggling to know the way, to remember the route
We think of how to find the point of debarkation.
We are now weak…subdued…jaded
Realizing the truth of our reality.
Do we continue to travail through life's journey
Or, afraid of the unknown,
Do we, like an ostrich, having no pride,
Fail to seek the intriguing experience?
Divorce is far too painful to ride.

Cleo E. Brown

Cleo E. Brown *(continued)*

The E. in my name stands for Elaine. Elaine is what I am called by my family and friends back home in California. In New York, however, everyone calls me Cleo. I am an educator as well as a writer, a poet, and a historian. I was educated in California at Bishop O'Dowd High School, California State University at Stanislaus, The University of California at Davis, and The University of San Francisco. My majors were history and education while my minor was political science. I have the equivalent of a PhD although the degree was never conferred. I do have a master's degree, however, from UC Davis. My belief in God is the center of my life; my children are also central to my being. God, my children, my family (parents and brothers) and friends as well as my cyclical belief in nature inspires my poetry.

All of a Sudden

All of a sudden, everything has changed
The moods, the smiles, the trees
The tempers, the oceans, the spirit
There is no peace, there is nothing to rejoice
There is no motto to restrain my sadness
I just know all of a sudden . . . everything has changed

All of a sudden what I love
Turns into a living hell . . . and there is the yell
Turn into a huge argue . . . and there is the face
Showing me, oh my! Showing me
That an argue can crown over that love
Once felt, once revered, once treasured

All of a sudden, everything has changed
And I do not know if this is for good or bad
And I do not know if it is worthy or worthless
And I found myself not knowing
What to do anymore
Once adored, once respected, once treasured

All of a sudden what I adore is not there
To take my hands and walk me out
To talk to me and make me dream
To take me to the moon
To recall me, how beautiful is a smile
To recall me the meaning of my companionship

All of a sudden, everything has changed
There is no fall, no summer
No spring and no winter in my heart
There is no hope that things like before will be
There is no certainty for the upcoming events
No meaning, no dream

All of a sudden, everything has changed
And I do not know what else to do
And the not knowing is the silent killer
Of my heart in love, once felt, once adored
Once priceless, once beloved
All of a sudden, everything changed

Lorena Soto

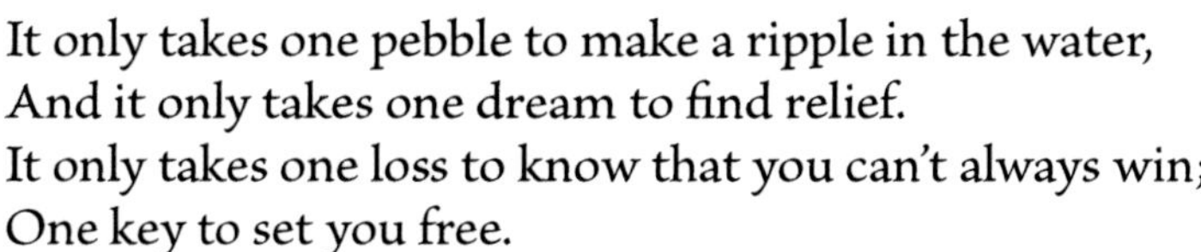

Over You

It only takes one pebble to make a ripple in the water,
And it only takes one dream to find relief.
It only takes one loss to know that you can't always win;
One key to set you free.

Now I'm no good at saying what I always need to say,
But a broken heart can't break so many times.
You led me down a long road and I don't know where we are.
I can't see through all your lies.

I can feel your breath under my skin
And I can feel the beat of your heart.
I can feel the Earth stop moving
As we reach for a new start.
But now you go back to your confusing moves,
So now I'm over you.

Too many songs play in my head and you fit every one.
You're handsome, but a beast shows underneath.
I played your game and lost because you cheated every round.
This puppet's gonna cut the strings.

I can feel your breath under my skin
And I can feel the beat of your heart.
I can feel the earth stop moving
As we reach for a new start.
But now you go back to your confusing moves,
So now I'm over .

You kiss me,
You leave me,
You love me,
You tease me;
But I won't go back to your bipolar moods

So now I'm over you.

Rebecca L. Martin

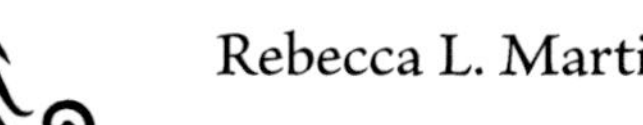

Rebecca L. Martin *(continued)*

Hello out there! My name is Rebecca Lynn Martin and since I can remember, I've always loved singing and acting. My love for poetry started when I was young and got angry at my mom. I went straight to my room and started writing until my hand cramped. It started off as silly poems about pizza or cats, but later they became more personal. With my poem "Over You," I had just gone through some stuff with this guy, and to forget about him, I combined my love for singing and poetry into a song. I never thought heartbreak could turn into such a great opportunity! I hope you like my poem!

The Devil's Ploy Song

Sing the song lifelong tears,
The weeping, wilted, wishful years.
Life is a domain scarce of truth,
As things so pure pass by the youth.

The tone changes in this song of soul.
The joyous, lovely, oblivious goal,
Still seeking the shine to the gem.
Hum your little humble hymn.

Cross my path of twisted rhythm.
You sneak your way until you schism.
As different sights and sounds of Devil,
Come whistling out in joyous revel.

End this song of being with a final swing.
The sighs and seems of youth to cling,
To naïve, unknowing notes of joy,
And the devil creates another ploy.

Katherine Turrentine

Enduring Our Freedom

On a bright September morn in New York City,
two American planes with terrorists aboard crashed
and downed the World Trade Center.
Oh God, what a pity . . .

Our lives have changed forevermore,
as our freedoms have been challenged . . .

These terrorists who dare to change our lives will never be.
Our hearts are strong, our defense is too as you will see . . .

President Bush has taken charge and taken flight
to send out soldiers into the night . . .

To get Bin Laden and his group of terrorists, our world
has come together to route out this man.
Now an anthrax scare poses another evil threat,
which will try to break us down.
Bin Laden, you monster, you deserve what you get . . .

This is not the Holy War that Bin Laden is trying to push.
We will have our freedoms thanks to our countrymen and
our president, George Bush.

Thanks to all freedom fighters who are helping the victims
of the tragedy of New York City.

Oleta P. Braley

My Heart Beats Content

You came upon my heart a vision yet to behold
A sound that was once hollow now delights within my soul
I set out on a path a true love God did send
I am enlightened by your presence my heart beats content

No longer strangers set adrift among the pages
A potential passion set to last long throughout the ages
Someone very kind honest and a truth is his intent
Came into my world my heart beats content

Your gentle embrace set a smile upon my face
A moment set in my heart allows the sunshine to take place
I will cherish each moment each hour is surely spent
My heart emits a different sound my heart beats content

As times goes on and love becomes our pleasure
We will grow in God's will for us our souls can only measure
Until a time we can again have moments that's are pleasing
My heart will beat fonder for you touch a sound not ceasing

My gentle thoughts they burn with the passion I feel for you
Deep down in my soul so warm and so true
My life no longer lonely a beautiful sentiment
My heart now wears a smile my heart beats content

Annalecia Holloway

Ms. Mikayla

Maybe I'm losing my mind
In some magnificent way,
Keeping me from a blind
And monotone world of gray.
Yelling out your whispered name
Like reading your unspeaking lips
And knowing I'm forever lame.

I love you like my faucet drips
(since I first saw it)

Ben Cross

Love Is the Answer
(What the World Needs Now)

Love is the answer
A magical potion of sorts
From sadness to joy
reversing sadness and doubt
during the worst of times

Through times unbearable
Love is the answer
Heartstrings ruptured and torn
Senses overwhelmed flounder
Seeking comfort and release

Spurned and cast aside
Loneliness and depression
Love is the answer
Look out from within
Retrieve faith, hope, ambition

Rebuke hatred and misdeeds
Ignore nefarious acts of others
Summon the light eternal
Love is the answer
Embrace all others as thyself

Enrich the world with daily deeds
Enter the spirit and soul of others
Allow intimacy without bounds
Without not feelings sincere
Love is the answer

Gary Stephen Weiner

Why

We are encouraged to ask questions
But when we question authority
We get punished.
Why?

We are encouraged to be ourselves
But when we go boldly
We are judged.
Why?

We are encouraged to try our best
But when we try to change things
We are hated.
Why?

When we are young
It seems our favorite word is why.
Why is the sky blue?
Why do birds sing?
Why are people so mean?
Our parents tell us we'll understand when we're older.
I'm older.
I'm still asking why.

Amber Davidson

KoKo

I'm like a cat when it comes to spring,
I lie outside and enjoy everything.
It starts with the sun warming up my back;
It fills me with calmness and laziness in fact.
Next come the clouds, puffy with joy;
I watch them shift, grow, and deploy.
I listen to trees as they ruffle their leaves,
And birds chirp away and like to sing through the day.
I smell fresh cut grass—already growing again.
I prowl through it crawling and prancing with grin.
The taste of a refreshing drink marks half my day;
I eat my tasty lunch and go back outside to play.
A light breeze picks up and tickles my face;
It plays with the plants and makes them dance with such grace.
There are blue, white and purple buds in bloom;
There are so many and they take up much room.
The water trickles with patterns or sickles;
Fish pop up and I hear the air they suck.
Smelling that barbeque is something, lo and behold,
You'll know it anywhere, age young into old.
Thus ends one of many spring days.
I like them like this and no other way.

Mikayla Degn

Happy Is What I'll Be

You give me butterflies.
You never ever tell me lies.
When you hold me tight,
I wanna stay that way all night.
All of these sweet kisses
under the star-lit sky
make me wanna hold you close
and kiss you on your nose.
Forever and a day
is how long I'm willing to stay.
As long as you love me
happy is what I'll be.

Jocelyn Myrick

Stupid Girl

He walked into your life
like he was straight out of a dream

You took his every word from the start
and you whole-heartedly believed

Stupid girl...
What were you thinking
he betrayed all your trust
Stupid girl...
how could you fail to see
he was damaging all your dreams
Stupid girl...

So tell me why it took so long
for you to finally see

There were only lies behind those eyes
and you never should have believed
Stupid girl...
dry your eyes
the damage has been done
Stupid girl...
the time will come
for you to fly once more
Stupid girl no more...never again.

Jennifer Cunningham

Guide Me There

For the winged angel that hath no flight
Now rest solicitous one
In tutelar form, I am your kite
Our journey hath just begun.

Sitting high a shoulder tall
With maimed a broken wing
Endear to you within my all
A requiem song you sing.

Unbeknownst with foehn wind
You breathe upon my ear
'Tis I you sing for of the end
Friendly slumber hath no fear.

Tis not the angel I am to carry
But the angel to be my guide
For the end that is to come for me
Even the angel could not hide.

Born to live upon this earth
Experience my greatest gift
Now born to die with all my worth
My head I proudly lift.

'Tis time we rent and time we lose
And for some is shorter than most
Now blithfully embracing untimely news
I'm guided by my host.

Oh little angel with broken wing
I've not wept nor have I pained
Let us fly and let us sing
For eternity I have gained.

Farida Pickett

I Know Where Beauty Lies

I know where beauty lies,
In brilliant cerulean skies,
In the euphony of lilting birdsong,
In trees, their mystic shadows leaning along.
Serene, stately leaf strewn lanes;
In beautiful music with its harmonious
Refrains.
In greenery upon majestic purple hills,
The melodic sweet song of the whippoorwills;
In the glorious radiance of the dawn,
In snowy cloud banks that are spawned
By the imminence of gathering rain;
In a mockingbirds voice lifted in soulful strain;
In the glorious majesty of this wondrous world
With its exquisite loveliness unfurled.

Glory Posey

Wilderness Angel

Moment of freedom
wilderness angel
muse of the deep northern forest
comes unto me as a queen
bare backed
on the gallop
of a sable stallion.
Nostrils mute
flare at her command!
Hoof beats halt
in the crisp white sand.
Dominion over the animals, she brings her soft-toned song.
A delicate violin string
harkening the heat of heart that makes the silkened grey sparrow sing,
I gently take her hand.
A forward bend,
glistening white skin,
thumb print dimples,
a natural entrance
to her sacred temple.
My strong hands stretch across her stately essence.
Mystery free
writhing ringlets of hair
gracefully
sweep the eternal sands.
Uninhibited!
Glancing eyes, curious at the laboring shadows,
engaged as a warm wave, gripping a steel pylon
forming a rhythmic L shape.
Hard to master, a deep fire burns.
Under the cool moon's willing eyes,
sunrise begins to ascend.
Fair maiden, will I see you again?

Gary Livingston

Still Standing

Here I am.
Standing here
Tall and proud
Here I am.
Telling you
Telling you out loud
That I survived
Through thick and thin
I may have gotten hurt,
But I am not broken.
I'm here today
To tell you my story
Of how I was beaten
And yet I still found glory.
I was taken hostage
And blinded by a mask.
I never knew
That I would have to do such a difficult task.
I was told lies
By the sincerest of eyes,
And as He struck his knife into me,
He slashed in all
directions.
And he continued to say
That it was a part of his affection.
He pushed me down,
And kicked me out,
He then turned around,
And left without a doubt.
He left me there to die,
Screaming in pain,
I was left to cry
In a pool of red rain.

I couldn't eat,
I couldn't sleep,
My heart was breaking,
With every last weep.
I'm surprised that I made it.
I thought that I wouldn't.
Everyone kept telling me,
Telling me I couldn't
But I guess you now know
That it all ended up being okay.
Otherwise,
I probably wouldn't be standing here today.

Alexis Worsley

Caged Within Darkness

Stricken with sickness you are left to die at hell's
bedrock,

Impatient you wither away in the labyrinth of your
heartless soul,

Lost you turn to the ones you once loved unknowing
they have cut the cord that held you to their hearts,

Helpless and alone your succumb to the darkness,

Soon you are swallowed by the depths of sadness
and regret,

Trapped in this endless maze you wonder searching for
the light that used to guide you,

Sinking into sadness you suffocate in your being,

Grasping for air you struggle to simply breathe giving
in the very shadow that surrounds you,

Engulfed by demons you fall victim to the evils inside you,

Weak with pain you try and stand on your feet but
are thrown to the ground,

Unable to stand you reach for the light and on your
knees you pray to be saved.

Natane Carrasco

Tristan

We keep looking everywhere,
but we don't see your face.
What happened? Where'd you go?
Is it too late to take your place?

We know all of those answers,
but something inside us begs to disagree.
It's hard realizing you're actually gone
when we didn't want you to leave.

Those days you were just missing,
it seemed unreal, like it wasn't true.
I'd hear some guys skating down the road
and check to see if it was you.

It never was you outside
and everyone is missing you so much.
I know if Heaven weren't so far away,
we'd never be out of touch.

So we'll hold onto the memories
to help us make it through.
We'll remember you making us laugh so hard
and we'll smile, thinking of you.

Courtney Marshall

Never Will I Know...

Never will I know the meaning behind your words,
Nor the feeling of your touch,
For never have I known you.

With hopeful eyes, I waited to see.
With hopeful ears I waited to hear.
But never have I known you.

Every confided word forever rings in my ears
As every harmonious melody eternally plays over again.
Still, never have I know you.

Now as I stare into your emerald gaze,
I realize the only truth I will ever know:
Never will I know you.

Chelsea Marsden

Father, I Miss the Days

Can't you see how much I need you,
but for support and encouragement, not the
discouragement that fills the scenes of my life.

Father, I miss the days
when you were impressed
by my achievements.

Now it's a matter of reflecting you,
not myself or anything I stand for,
but who you want me to be.

Father, I miss the days
when you supported me
for who I am inside.

Father, what happened
to the love and respect
you used to show?

It'll be hard to watch you disappear
from my life and from my thoughts.
I've always been your little girl, but
that has to change just as you have.

Amanda Pidlisny

Beautiful or Man-Made

It's when minds distort to see beauty
That sadness comes into play
When the black rose is turned to blue
The earth turned to grey
When the background life is blurred
So that you see beyond your face
That's when beauty's buried
And tears appear in place.

A tarnished cold deteriorated a flowing soul inside
Freezing it to make up for the black hole it leaves behind
A rose becomes a statue for only people to admire
With merely our eye—without scent or desire.

Why do we refurbish the world
With such simulated splendor?
Beauty wouldn't have a price
If only we'd surrender
To the way it's meant to be—
The way the world was designed;
But then I guess the world made man
To change what nature had in mind.

Munawwar Abdulla

Moving On

The days of a child are hard to remember
It's full of fun and play
No responsibility or worry
Life is easy as a child
but life moves on

Going through stages of life
You change to fit the stage
Learning and growing throughout life
Leads up to year eighteen
Then life moves on

At eighteen you are an adult
Done with high school
Going to college or future endeavors
So stressful and you're not out yet
But life moves on

Figuring out what to do
Seems so easy but isn't
What can I do to decide?
I have to choose
For life to move on

Alisha Ellis

Untitled

He remembers the day he saw her
The first time they met
What she was wearing
He doesn't forget
Looks at her like no one else does
There's something about him
She doesn't know what
But something about him
She completely loves and trusts
He still looks on watching from afar
Waiting for this girl who's stolen his heart.
Something about her this boy knows
It's that something about her why
He never lets go
Holds on tries to keep her close
But can't say what it is he feels most
Instead haunting her like a ghost
Doesn't always say much
But he's said enough
To make her hold on even though
She feels so rough
Loves him and really does care
He does too but is still fighting himself
Wondering do I dare?
He struggles with himself deep within
All because he's afraid to let love in.

Stephanie Craig

Three Simple Words

Three words, three simple words and that will be a step closer to her.
She could be your hand to hold, the one you shelter from the cold. The
bold embers enhance her beauty and set your heart a flame. Your love
burns for the one thing you can't have.

Three words, three simple words that could be the end to everything
   you know.
You're never the first choice but maybe this time you won't be chosen
last. Maybe they will finally listen to your voice, what you have to say,
and not laugh at the displeasure you have brought upon them.

Three words, three simple words and she might just say them back.
Maybe this time your not losing the game. Maybe for once you're in
first place and maybe, just maybe, those dreams that fill your childish
mind can come true. There is a chance, a chance, that your heart aches
for the same thing, each other.

Three words, three simple words that now haunt your every waking
   breath.
For she holds hands with another. That step that you took didn't bring
you any closer. Go shelter yourself in your fantasies because she will
never choose you, it will always be him. Make your departure, walk
away. Those three simple words you had to say have been broken down
by the goodbye she tossed your way. Go be Romeo without your Juliet
and drink your poison. Say those three simple words that finalize the
end of you,
"Goodbye, my love."

Julia Parham

The Kiamichi

In the upper reaches of Oklahoma's Kiamichi Mountains a river is
Born. Along its banks grow groves of pine, cedar, ash, dogwood and
fields of corn.

Far below in the land of the Choctaw a drama drawing diverse actors is
staged and shallow shoals of river rocks gurgle and dance from endless
days.

In former days the brown-skinned hunters often dogged their prey
Where panther, fox, deer, bobcat, bear, and rabbits played.

In later days a farmer drove team and wagon into waters above, deep,
the teams to drink, the iron wheel rims to shrink, their grip to keep.

Another group is lured to the spot to take their summer break,
To camp on the high bank with the scene below, as one's dreams may
make.

No water so clear, so sweet, so cool, as nature's spring nearby,
No air so fresh so clean as from cane breaks the river goes by.

The sounds of all the flopping fish and tree frog songs at night,
Mixed with locusts, crickets, and some unknown bugs that bite.

The magic of this magnate thus appeals to folks of every kind,
To swim or fish, or paint the scene, or stroll through tree and vine.

To overcome a lack of late
How great a place to meditate.

Beside the quiet flowing stream that tends to cast a spell,
The smoke from fire that stings our eyes, but wood we love to smell.

The tent that leaks and ruins our sleep from unexpected showers,
We tolerate and cannot wait to tell about this trip of ours.

No medicine that's compounded by man can make us feel so good,
For sure, as trees and streams and skies and seas, or God, who has the
    cure.

"The heavens declare the glory of God," a writer of Psalms has said,
For Nature is a sign, at best, to point us to the son, who led.

The river of life that flows on high is in the revelation,
The river below, he leads us to know the joy of our salvation.

However long, however far, the Kiamichi river may flow,
Can never compare with the maker up there who meets our needs
    below.

Bobby Spear

Letter from a Stranger

Dear old woman
dead for ages,
here is your letter,
yellowed pages.

Telling of common
good old things,
of happiness, sorrow
life always brings.

Thanking for money
begging for news
of beloved sister
hated to lose.

Love you, dear ghost
old woman of mine,
you speak to me
from the edge of time.

Telling me things
I should know,
showing the way
before I go.

Sweet old woman,
gone for years,
your letter tells of
…hopes and fears,

When your own world
was sad and gay,
but all that now
has passed away,

And you are now
what I'll soon be,
A soul en route
to eternity.

Doris Beier

The Girl Behind the Red Door

Yelling,
Screaming.
She hears this every day.
She hurts,
She cries.
Her tears stain her pink cheeks.
She didn't know what to do,
Until she found you.
Yes you.
You saved her.
You gave her a loving home with two baby boys.
And her parents yelling and screaming,
Is not more.
She is no longer the girl behind the red door.

Julia Laude

If Not for God

Sometimes, when I look around and see
Spectacular displays of ever-changing scenery,
With many delicate and vibrant hues of color,
And gaze upon the quiet beauty of the perfect rose,
I ask myself, how could all this beauty be
If not for God?

Sometimes, when I feel the warmth and see
The soft glow of the radiant sun,
Shiver in the coolness of the crisp moonlight evening,
Feel the wet softness of the gentle rain,
I wonder in awe where this creativity would come from
If not for God.

Sometimes when I think about the mystery of our being,
The wonder of our joys, the sadness of our sorrows,
Or the enriched fulfillment of bearing a child
And knowing the love He gives that we feel,
I think to myself, we would not have such meaning
If not for God.

Christine E. Antall

Peace of Mind

A life that is filled with peace
And joy is the only way to live,
So end each day with just one
Thing:
Forgive, forgive, forgive.

Each one of God's creations
Do things we should not do.
We all have times we really need
Someone to forgive us too.

When you get older you will find
A special gift is peace of mind.
You find it when you learn to live
With a loving heart
That will forgive.

God loves you in a special way
We're told we must love this way
To forgive all wrongs and you will find
God's special gift—peace of mind.

June L. McNeely

Remember

We must remember what's been done,
By someone's daughter, someone's son.
They've paid their price for liberty,
The awful cost of being FREE!
The lives we've lost in war a given,
Courage they've faced is always proven;
What they have done for our security,
Must never fade from our memory.
Remember all the wars they've fought,
Let not their lives be lost for naught!
Let all who stood on freedom's line
Stay in our prayers, our hearts, our minds!
We hope we'll live our lives in peace,
And pray that soon all wars shall cease!
We know that God will surely bless,
All who died protecting us.
So place your flowers upon their graves,
And remember all the lives they've saved!
Let's pray that God will protect and care
For all who still serve anywhere!

Gary L. Barnett

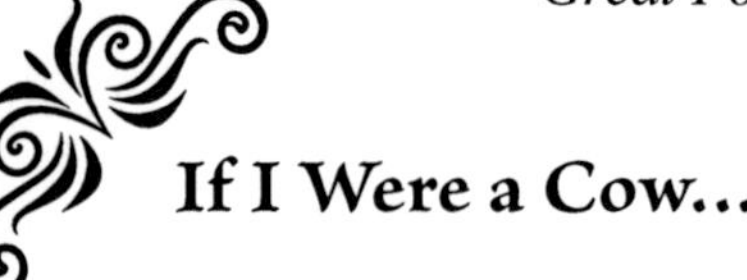

If I Were a Cow…

If I were a cow...
I'd certainly jump and moo.
I'd also do all the things
That "human beings do."
I'd laugh, giggle and yodel too—
I'd dance and sing the whole day through.
I'd fly right up to that big round moon
Without the likes of rockets and wings.
I'd check out that age old rumor…
The moon is made of cheese—
And I'd be big and warm on my fur coat
As warm as warm could be!

Forget that "How-Now-Brown-Cow" stuff
And all that educated bunk.
I'd be the first "All-American-cow"
To just go punk!
I'd be purple, red, orange and green
I'd be the most marvelous cow you've ever seen!
My eyes would glisten … on my tail I'd wear a yellow ribbon.
And if I like you lots, I'd walk with you
And to your worldly problems listen.
But of course, I'd flip my tail
And fill your pail
With the best of milk you've ever drank!

No don't go callin' me "No Bossy Cow."
I'll call you sweetheart and you can call me Al.
Oh, but of course, we'll be the best of pals.
And when it comes to dancin' … I'd hoof it up in a chorus line
I would moo-moo and in my zest my four legs would be a flyin'
And as you can plainly see …
There never ever could have been or ever even will be …
A cow just like me!

Terrence L. Johnson-Cooney

His Embrace

Sleeping deeply, to escape the pain.
My wilted yearning to reclaim his
embrace, if only once more to see
his face.
Saturated with emptiness, all I
feel is complete sadness. Longing to
be engulfed in his core, if only
once more.
Deeply sleeping, hoping to awake
finding this heartache all a big
mistake.
Feeling as I am awake…somehow
changing fate he is here with me.
So real, I feel him wrapping his
arms around me so tightly.
Quickly, I turned to look into
his eyes. The coveted embrace
vanished as I opened my eyes.
A disseminated flash of a sweet
dream crashed.
Devastated…I weep…tormented!
I cannot go back to sleep. There…
is where I felt his last embrace, if
only I had not turned to see his
face… Aaron 27, never to see 28.

Lisa A. Miller

Every Day

The lady that you're given me is the one I've been lookin' for.
The day that we become just one, I will love her deep from head to toe.
I think she put a spell on me, she's always runnin' through my mind.
I wanna love her all my life, until the very end of time.
I think I had to run away, because you found me by myself.
I wanna treasure all of our love, so I can put you back on my shelf.
Is she the love I'm lookin' for, so I can love her in every way?
I wanna hold her in my arms, and squeeze her body, really tight every
    day.

Thomas L. Smith

The Beauty of Flowers

Summer flowers blowing in the breeze,
Soon winter will be here and the ground will freeze.
Get ready to plant your seeds in the fall
So that your flowers will be ready to grow big and tall.
The winter snow will keep them warm and safe
Till the snow is gone and are ready to face
The world above and find their place
To show their beauty with love and grace.
Then spring will be over and summer will begin.
You start the new season to plant seeds again.
These flowers will grow big and strong
With the fragrance you'll love all summer long.

Carmella F. Smith

Crucifixion

The cruel nails pierce His hand
As blows of hammer fill the air
And darkness stretches o'er the land.

God's angels awe the blood-soaked sand
That trickles from the thorn-braced hair.
The cruel nails pierce His hand.

Both John and Mary bravely stand
With pious women weeping there
And darkness stretches o'er the land.

His cross is raised as wicked planned;
He prays His Father these to spare.
The cruel nails pierce His hand.

Rough soldiers guard, nor understand
What innocence this cross does bear,
And darkness stretches o'er the land.

As long ago in Heaven planned
For sins of man He makes repair.
The cruel nails pierce His hand,
And darkness stretches o'er the land.

Edward J. Schlossman

Mirror Image

My mother told me about "the old woman
Who lived behind her mirror."
She said the hag looked like her.
Sadie always made up stories.
She played roles.
She stole good lines—
That one from a French play.
It isn't life.

Now the crone is behind my mirror.
Odd how she looks so much like me.
It doesn't seem right.
Old ladies always live in shoes,
The "fairest of them all" in mirrors.
Sadie taught me those fairy tales too.
How could I know
She played smoke and mirrors
With the truth?

After all, it isn't life! Is it?

Eileen Z. Cohen

Cliché

You and I were one in the same cliché.
Different ages of love flowed from feelings of enrapture.

Time satisfied our longing only with chance meetings.
I could see the candlelight burning bright—
in your eyes—forlorn.

And every once in a while, magic briefly came to stay,
allowing special out-of-the-way places to be born.
Where happiness from the stars covered us in delight,
leading us to travel the road of twilight
where paths appeared—
then quickly vanished,

as fate hunted us down, caught in the moment,
separating the outside, keys of our lives,
though never reaching the inner voices—
holding the never-ending spirit
of our souls.

Nicolette R. Arrigo

Untitled

I've loved you since we were in school
And couldn't wait to marry you.
Then orders came—I couldn't stay
Found out I had to go away.

I'm now a soldier in Iraq,
Walking around with my backpack.
I'm fighting with the enemy
Because that's where I need to be.

I am a man who totes a gun,
I'll fight this war until it's won.
But homebound's where I want to be,
Holding my children on my knee.

Be face to face with you—my wife
To get back to a normal life.
I lie awake on my bedroll
Wanting to touch your very soul.

You don't get too far from my sight—
I kiss your picture every night.
I keep it tucked inside my cover,
I miss you so much my sweet lover.

I wrote a letter just today—
By noon it will be on its way.
When you see just the way it's signed,
You'll know you're always on my mind.

I pray at night on bended knee
That I'll soon see my family.

Kathy Silva

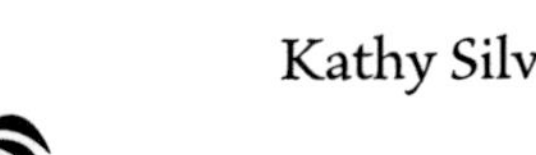

Powerfully Insane

My face wet from the tears I cry,
a face of entrapment by my own doing.
My inner soul repressed and defined by the choices I made.
I swallow this grief and digest in my body inspiring a powerfully insane
    mind.
I am financing my wet face to be a true reflection of what is trapped
    inside.

I dream and fantasize about the death of the ego.
Many days I long to push pride aside just to piss my ego off.

Yet, in my awakened life or illusions of life all I do is loath to a pathetic
    melody that plays along with my sad song.

Nothing can be just what it is.
It becomes a patriotic ego party fixed on what it thinks it should be.
The ego in my life so arrogantly examples a faulty love and together we
    drink to my intoxication and physical death. Cheers!

In my cold icy voices I slur out "pour some out for me, brother!"
Kill this need to be awake because we fight and want to destroy our
    higher self that was created to be.
Being powerfully insane I scream, "Take the shank away from me!"
Here I am in a powerfully insane jail that my ego has created just for
    me.

De'Anna Quillen

Tin Floor Requiem

Pit. Pat.
On that silver-cobalt mat
She debuts a worn leather sole sonata

The ones whom she moves with those pale carnation shoes
Loiter no longer to be able attest
For they are far and away, gone forth by the arc and sway
Of her frail, famished bodice

The skip of her feels and stoical, swan-like neck
Brings motion to a capacious auditorium
The slice and slash of the strewn sediment of ash
Shed my miss
They become in trance by the trailing, faint hiss of her dance
Singing a scene on that blank canvass for all and for each

Ah! They adore and begin to weep for a share of the passion beheld
    by her
Like the flit of a monarch's wings on a molten, grey pond
And a flick of compassion thrown in the eyes of loss
From the warm radiance of a wielding heart, whole again,
before their drawn, sodden apparitions

A final bid for one fully became their own,
unto them by an ornate tear cascading her fair ivory cheek
In an absence came the vanquish of a new sun
Fed to her so that it may be for all
Not solely a condolence for one

And so one's fruit became a banquet for all on that afternoon of a single
    spirit's ball
A calm, agile row she procured to ponder
To a new day she fears not to wander

Where no bleary salutations she is endowed to compose
Where she need not to mourn through a graveyard prose
Or wish upon the bedrock of a dream

Yes, here she flees with the feet of a strong veteran's heart
There she paints for the liberty of her own
Then
There
She need not steer abroad
That place where
She need not dance alone

Brianna V. Mahon

Three Practicals

Intelligence is this, having the ability to learn, now
Cope with learning, without a formal education. Wow!
And have that certain amount of mentality, brain-power
To be certain of yourself always, using wit, every hour
Be sure of information, using acumen or the spreadings
Spreading news intelligently and always with tidings
Show your intelligence by acting out with some sense
Use good sense with mother-wit; do not appear dense

Knowledge having the information or the education
Education, information needed for knowledge is action
When you acquire knowledge, it is like having evidence
Evidence, like a testimony, a sure case or idea whence
Whence is a source? You receive it from what or where
And you have knowledge; you know how much you care
Putting knowledge together is mind-boggling. It's a lot of acts
You now have knowledge, and then you gather all facts

Insight it is a look into a long word; it's intuitiveness
Look yes, we need more insight on this topic, directness
The word insight is used, people say, it's a second sight
Is that so? I don't know. It is more of a sixth sense, right?
So, thinking right is used; think of the word immediately
Insight carries with it, also signification and this, stately
Intelligence, knowledge, insight, a terrific combination
Intelligence, knowledge, insight known as gratification

Clarence L. Hammonds

At this time, I am composing my 1,490th poem. I began writing poems in 1944 while stationed in India during WWII. I write these kinds of poems—pantoum, free verse, sonnets, Shakespearian sonnets, and rhyming poems. I have four degrees. I am eighty-seven years old and was married sixty years, then my wife died. I have a son and daughter, four grands, and three great-grands. My son encourages me to keep writing. He has a doctorate degree and has bound all of my poems in three three-ring binders. I leave my apartment daily for Starbucks, to write.

'Til Then

Through misty eyes I saw you wave
As your ship took you out to sea.
Though six months you will be away,
Your treasured love will stay with me.

So precious are my memories
Of the time we have had together.
The laughter and the fun we shared
In every kind of weather.

In the storms we looked for rainbows
And in the sunshine we would play.
We were duly blessed with a lasting love,
For our God had shown us the way.

I will write you every day,
And I shall be forever true.
Keep these words inside your heart,
I need you, I miss you, I love you.

Phyllis J. Mattice

Thankful Writer

I am so thankful to be a writer!
It's a talent I've been told.
Also it helps me to express things in life
before I'm very, very old!
I've written many things
that have been published near and far,
but I've not yet become rich
or even a movie star.
Although if very successful
my talent of writing could go far,
if one needed only a sponsor
who would choose who it seems?
It takes faith, talent, and a dreamer of things,
and when one really searches the heart,
the riches come deep inside ourselves.
There's even those cherished memories
that come in "flashbacks" as they last.
Some are of the past, present, and now.
Just what about our futures yet?
I've written things short and long
and hope someday for the best.
There's a lot of things in life
that are a challenge and a test.
I've completed short stories and songs,
and poetry at my best and pray God tells
me what to say as a thankful writer for today!

Frances E. Camp

My Hawk

Don't tell me there's no Heaven
No reason to aspire,
I know my spirit love
Soars over, higher and higher.

I like to sit beneath the heavens
Watching clouds play in the sky,
Then silently a hawk appears
You're watching me, you didn't die.

I see this hawk most every day.
He's circling, circling overhead.
I know you always wished to fly,
What more is there to be said?

Bernice K. Flannery

A Heart of Sorrow

Upon this hill, looking over the valleys, tears are falling upon my chest. As I stand here broken-hearted there is no rest, no peace, and no calmness. No repose for my torn heart is to be realized for the realization of what is lost cannot be recommenced.

A heavy sigh and a blink of the eye cannot stop the water as it outward flows. The pain, anger, and sadness abundant will not stop for the soul controls it. The mind is in a confused state, attempting to rationize, understand, and move forward. It has great pause, as existence itself cannot piece it together.

Why, why, why is always the word of question.
 Ah, alas, to no avail, the answer vestiges unknown.

Pamala D. Adams

A Walk Through McDonough Park

A walk through McDonough Park can be a transporting experience, at
least I have found it so.
The trails of McDonough Park in the early spring or late fall and
winter months are less traveled and one has an increased likelihood of
traversing them in silence and solitude.
I remember during the fall on an overcast and particularly windy day,
just before a rainstorm, the leaves being hurled in endless cascades
across the trail and the branches of trees being bent to and fro with
force from the fierceness of the wind.
In the midst of this Aeolian tempest, the trail tortuously wends its way
beneath overhanging and tumultuously swaying tree limbs that seem to
create a tunneling to some dark and turbulent place.
The colorful warmth of fall colors muted by the saturnine appearance
of clouds of varying chiaroscuro shades that greatly dim the light and
herald an imminent storm, and yet all of it is purely beautiful and you
realize you are immersed in a living canvas . . . Of sheer perfection.

Of course, there is no walk through McDonough Park like a walk when
it's raining.
The resounding orchestration of raindrops against the leaves with the
almost tympanic punctuations and crescendos of the wind creates such
inexpressibly beautiful sounds.
The woods can also be darker at these times, as well as more quiet,
with the sound of the raindrops bounded by stillness and silence that
easily becomes suffused into oneself so that the frenetic pace is slowed,
harsher inner voices fade, and quieter ones speak that are more easily
heard in such silence.
A kind of communion occurs between the inner and the outer, spun by
the latter, a gift from McDonough Park.
A gift that reminds me…a walk through McDonough Park can be such
a transporting experience
Oh, I have found it so…I have found it so.

Fred Thomas Lee

Look Into Me

Look into my eyes, and say to my face you'll be fine
Look closer into my soul
And tell me everything will be okay
Look closer into my heart
And tell me it's never been broken
Look closer at me
You'll eventually see a person falling
Look closely at who I am
Don't say you know who I am
Because you never will
I look into your eyes
And I see a liar
I look into your soul
I see a traitor
I look at your heart
It is pure black
I look closer at you
I see a false advertisement
I look closely at who you are
I know what you are
Others must be warned
Hurting others
You must be forgotten.

Meghan Young

Typhoon Dissolved

My autism kicks in
I couldn't make eye contact and I didn't like to be touched
Occupational therapy helped me outgrow that
Now I can make eye contact with someone close

I can now make human contact
As I was growing a bit older, the inner storm was forming
This typhoon made me throw tantrums and fits
People didn't want to be around me
One day, I was put on better medication

When I was ten years old, the typhoon dissolved
Swell, that solves my autism problems
I am no longer a severe autistic kid having a typhoon fit
Thank goodness…the typhoon dissolved just in time

Michael Nohilly

I am Michael James Nohilly, a sixteen-year-old, high-functioning autistic teenager. I lived in New York City for fifteen years until I moved to Orange County, NY. I've written poetry for about eight years. My early poems were kiddy, meaning I didn't understand much about poetry. Eight years later, I've written fifty poems for them to be published and I've published poetry in some contests.

Rainy Days

I love to sit out in the rain, only God can see my pain.
When it starts I run outside, sit on the ground stare at the sky.
Watching the water all around, feeling my tear rolling down.
My skin is moist, cloths are drenched, but I hardly notice it.
I only see the things I've done, to make you mad and make you run.
The rain has stopped I go inside, everyone looks at me this time.
Do they know I cried?

Brianne McKenzie

Pride

No season should bare a treason,
This country is my family, my life, and my home.
A home with sturdy walls,
Food and protection.
With my freedom alive,
Never going to die,
American pride I hold.
Never disappointing,
Always supporting.
Pearl Harbor can't wreck us,
911 can't shut us down.
We are United,
We are States,
We are America.
Land of the free,
Home of the brave.

Chloe Criez

Alone

Nobody knows what I've been through
Nobody knows my shame

Nobody knows what I go through
Or that I'm the one I blame

Nobody knows my struggles
Or my fights through daily life

Nobody understands me
And I handle it in strife

Nobody knows the real me
Or the worries I go through

Nobody really loves me
Or wants what I want too

Nobody appreciates me for me
Or accepts who I am

Nobody respects what I do
Or that I have a plan

Nobody knows the real me
Or all that I can be

Nobody knows what I'm worth
I'm just waiting for someone to see

Natasha Marshall

Natasha Marshall *(continued)*

I am a freshman at Miami University of Ohio studying chemistry and psychology as my majors. I aspire to be a pediatric oncologist. I am the daughter of Tanya and Chris Marshall and sister to Brittany Boden, Christopher Marshall and Alyssa Marshall. I use my poetry as a stress and emotion release. When writing, I hope to relate to my audience in many ways and make sure they know they are not alone in what they are going through. I sincerely hope people enjoy my poetry as much as I enjoy writing it.

Her Final Act

After she's been through hell,
she found it hard to tell.
The earth and sky meet,
as the ground disappears from beneath her feet.
On either side, a black wall,
as she endures this perilous fall.
Her life has been drained,
the sky cried, it rained.
The fallen angel knew
as she went to
take her last stand
against the deadly hand.
Now for all to remember
on that fateful night last December,
the curtain forever drawn, this is a fact,
at the end of her final act.

Keely Blank

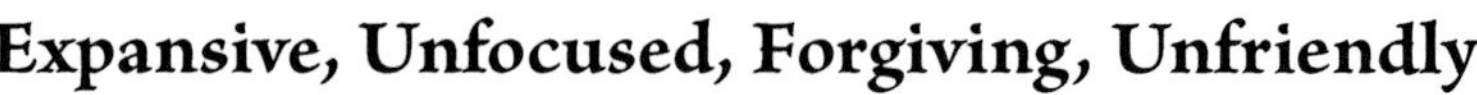

Expansive, Unfocused, Forgiving, Unfriendly

With wine in her hair and strawberry blond in her eyes
Head low, grown chesty, barefooted, dressed cheaply
Reenacting cruise control with Oakland pie and apple soul
Caramelizing the pendulum bells in the Aberdeen the Avon women sell
And you may ask how you can turn kerosene to caramel

There are cuffs on his wrists so they match hers tonight
And those small silver rings say they weren't brought up right
Man clad in authority, allow her to crumble 'neath your seniority
Mercy please, mercy please, as she drowns in humiliation and inferiority
I'll spit out the words, then she'll ask about and hate them
They are the closest composition to meeting my proud, flexed position

Robed in white, there she sits with fruit in her hand
Then clenching her thighs, adorned by feeble, blank command
Tell her that she did nothing wrong, he just needed to move on
He needed someone else in somewhere else where he belonged
Her ladylike words would cradle him in soft addiction
While he breathed syllables into eighteen-hour fiction

She only wanted to know what he spurned
He spurned her, then he burned
And grew out of a face which he snubbed out, wiped off, replaced
It follows her to bed and she paints it on her ears
She holds the words in her mouth and prints them on her fears
There are fanged-out, blow-dried, free-willed, cat-eyed women smoking
Inside her head as if it's midnight in New York City

We want to know if she can melt her spirit down like butter
And pour it over the people
We want to know if she can be a seabird agent,
Comprehend apricots with blackmail and bleachers.

Lynn Mireault

A Thousand Timid Trepidations

A thousand timid trepidations cloak
My every stunted thought and stammered speech—
If so afflicted were the roots of oak
As I, they'd falter from the water's reach.
And so, a seed that might've been a tree
Would crumble into desiccated mud.
For what? The fear that nothing flows in thee
From which a seed could grow into a bud?
I know the nonsense as it leaves my lips,
For I can see it brimming from your eye
On down your rosy cheeks and rolling hips—
Enough to feed a meadow to the sky!
Alas, I cast my dreams back up above,
And silently entreat you for your love.

Nathan Copperwheat

Music Forever

Singing with a passion means the heart no longer is confided to your
    body
The music comes easily without fault or hesitation
Mind opens up, heart grows wings
And it flies to a majestic world of song

The notes dance a ballet on the tongue,
Technique improves every day of practice
Voice grows louder, simultaneously lungs grow stronger
Soul becomes one with the song

A place where every word holds a special meaning
Every breath and beat tells a story
Not singing in hopes of riches or fame
But singing for love, peace, and joy

The room disappears as soon as the song begins
Freeing the imagination to soar
Opening the door to the very soul
Slaughtering the feeling of shyness and shame

In a world of dreams one lets the voice take them away
Where the heart and song rule all
Marking life with the handprint of music
This is where the spirited belong
Singing with a passion means the heart speaks, not the tongue
Yes, this is truly where the spirited belong

Gwen Rose Quill

I have been writing for as long as I can remember; whenever I feel low or bored or just plain filled with inspiration, I like to pick up a pen and paper and start writing poetry. Poetry really inspires me, because it's basically just pouring your heart out onto paper and I absolutely love doing that. There are no real rules that you have to follow and no one looking over your shoulder telling you when you can or can't write. To me, music and poetry are the same; they both come from the heart and I feel free participating in both. Writing and singing have been passions of mine for as long as I can remember, and they will always hold a special place in my life and in my heart.

My Last Goodbyes

One day in July,

I thought my dad was telling a lie,
at the time I was only seven,
I couldn't believe he had gone to Heaven.

I never thought I'd be that sad,
when all I ever was, was glad,
they said he slipped away that night,
he went away to see the light.
My tears spilt over my eyes,
as I gave him my last goodbyes,
upon hiss cold cheek I gave a kiss,
because he is someone I would dearly miss.
He was gone like the wind,
our memories in my mind are pinned,
I really truly miss him,
without him here my life seems dim.
I wish he were still here,
still breathing this atmosphere, I miss his smile,
I still shed a tear once in a while.
I never thought I'd see him again,
but I dream of him now and then.
That one night in my dream,
I thought I was going to scream,
I saw him standing there,
his eyes full of care.
I hope he will soon visit,
and I'm sure I won't miss it,
one day he will come back,
but until then I'm keeping track.

Natalina Zieman

Prufrock on My Mind

Words are tricky.

You can't sit in silence, yet somehow it envelops you,
It can be louder than a punk rock concert
And consume you.
The unsaid words can sometimes be the most haunting of all.
The unwritten words are worst.

My words to me are never going to be
The same to someone else.
"I am not Prince Hamlet," and I'm not even J. Alfred Prufrock.
If I could just speak to
One
Person and have them hear me,
Would it be enough?

If I had one more day in London, would it be enough?
Would it even matter to anyone?
I have a mute voice that wants to sing.

Emily Walker

When I Die (Sarasota, FL)

When I die
I will float down Main Street
With the crowds at the galleries.
I will drift into the Opera House courtyard
And mingle with the patrons around the little fountain there.
I will mix myself
With the tangy Gulf mist that smells of salt and far places
And create rainbow auras around the streetlights.
When I die
I will finally be an irrevocable part of this place:
People will report a wraith at Five Points Park
Dancing among the sculptures.
Don't be alarmed—
It'll only be me
When I die.

Stephanie Bashein Emerson

Mama

Mama we have not always been close
but over the years we became close
like butter on toast
I been by your side since 2005
when you became disabled I promise
I will always be here for you
until your eyes close forever
I love you so much thank God
He is keeping you and still blessing you
I know the road we've been on has not
always been easy but still yet we
are making it
I call you a miracle lady doctors
gave up on you thought you'd
be dead and gone
but you're still here keeping your
head up and holding on
I am glad that you are my mama
you always believe in me
so loving and caring
Back in the days I thought you
were hard on me growing up
Now as I look back I see you
was doing your job I understand
now I want to say thank you
I wouldn't change you for nothing
in this world I love you Mama
always and forever

Angelita J. Dixon

Love

Please take care of me
Each and every day
And look after me
Not to ignore me
Until the day pass
That I am not here
But I will love you
Until that day comes
That I will live on
Together with you
Every single day
Remembering you!

Carissa Rubin

The Wish Behind My Rainbow

It's not my heart, to make man cry,
But have you seen their true deny?
The rainbow waits, to see their faith,
Their willingness, to sing "How Great".

In valleys deep, the rainbow flies,
I'm wishing, not a cloud rolls by,
But set upon my clear blue skies,
Is Heaven's sent, I will supply!

I'll tell you, how I wished they hear,
To keep their faith, and boot their fear!
The joy of Christ, outdoes the storm,
When nothing works, the rainbow's born!

The kingdom waits! I cherish you!
With Father's love, and rainbows too!
In precious want, they fill the sky,
With artist named, he's answered "why".

Why do opened, see my rainbows?
There's blessed hope, 'tween you and me.
A perfect peace surrounds my rainbows,
They'll be more for you to see!

My jealous warns, surround my wish,
Telling lost, my bold insists,
That manners meet, at rainbows end,
With God's renew, and prayers sent.

When distance finds my rainbow's glare,
Keep these words of mine to share,
It's the Christ, at work today,
Mending hearts, who've lost their way.

Across the Father's deep blue skies,
A glowing arch of colors fly,
He's etched our faith with promise there,
He handles all, there's none compare!

Faye A. Deller

New Directions

The hopeful butterfly looks up to the sky
That beautiful combination of blue and purple
Swirling in patterns of delicate beauty
Breathing in a sigh of relief
The butterfly flutters his wings, taking in
The excitement of his wild, peaceful world
This world that contains hunters and prey
Families and friends, the world that he
Goes to for comfort, for simple pleasures
The butterfly lets the rays of the sun
Light up the colors of his wings
Cascading those colors to the floor for the
Creatures to dance and laugh in
He takes flight as the leaves rustle with
New found energy, his wings slapping at
The wind as he glides effortlessly through the
Delicious air, tasting every new sensation
As he heads toward his new destination
Mind prepared and eyes focused
His emotions ready for a new direction

Amanda L. Eckmann

Darkness Against the Shining Light

Day by day the darkness falls
As it fades the light will show
Ready, set, let us fight
Know their strength, know their might
Never let them take me down
Everlasting screams and shout
So caught up in this battle
So longing to end this shadow
All our soldiers painted red
Growing closer, more drop dead
As they strike a spirit flies
Into the light shaded gray
Never see the light of day
Songs of life, the angels sing
Towards their king, sword we swing
Turn our backs to the demons
Holding on till the end
Enter battle with no fear
Shining blades held so tight
High above the faeries fly
Into the fire, ice we throw
Now we rise, down they go
Imagine a world unbroken
Now we end these pools of crimson
Give up, go back, leave this world alone
Let us leave this blood-soaked field tonight
Is this the true end for us to say goodbye
Go and stand to the other side
Hold on to hope and we can end the lies
Time to bring back our long lost light again

Tiffany A. DeGarmo

For Those Who Didn't Make It

For those who didn't make it
Are those left behind
For those who deserve better
When times are not so fine

A rape victim left for dead
Genocide because of religion
Raging wars instead of negotiations
Because of different region

Remember those who died
Whether on ground or in the sky
Those who've done nothing wrong
And were left to die

Recall those for sacrifice
To save others for to live than perish
To think better for the next generation
That was their only wish

A decade after that dreadful day
A day that leaves us in tears
A day we shall never forget and live in infamy
No matter how many years

For those who do make it
Be happy with what you've got
Don't receive forget-me-nots

Thanks to those who are empathic
For those who care
Those who compromised a crisis
For those split in half and share

Life isn't fair
Trust me, it isn't
So, remember those
For those who didn't make it

Ashley Holady

Angry Eyes of the Hold on Combat Soldier

His eyes never change,
That empty angry stare.
That look took him from here to there
No one's seeking the blame.
They can't even tame their own brains.
The infantry GI's recognize each other;
They nod at one another as they pass by,
Secretly holding back the tears in their eyes.
Silence is their best friend.
Others can't see where they've been.
Some don't dream for years.
Then something comes from deep within their fears.
All of a sudden, their nightmares are here.
Suddenly they feel they're back there again.
When will this angry feeling end?
From war to war, when can the soldier begin to live again?
They wrestle in their sleep, the ones who come back home.
They are fighting the change over zone.
The world they live in, we can't attend.
The world we live in, we can't defend.
When two worlds collide, it's quite a sorrow.
For those who won't let them borrow, there may be no tomorrow.
They need your energy to help them survive.
For those who don't give of themselves are barely alive.
To the combat soldier, we hold you to our hearts.
Forever and ever, we will never part.

Eleanor P. Atzert

I Don't Understand

I don't understand…
why Eve bit the apple
why king Herod was so merciless to a baby
why Jesus didn't call on the angels in his last hours
But most of all…
why people don't practice what they preach
why Christ is being taken from CHRISTmas
why God bothers to love me so much
What I understand…
is that He does love me
is that I don't deserve his love and mercy
is that I shouldn't understand it all

Kealy Wassil

I have been writing poems since sixth grade. Sometimes my poems are sad, others are joyous, but they are almost always about God. I participate in band, basketball and softball and try to give the glory to God, no matter what the situation. This is why I write poems and songs to give praise to the one who gives me all of my gifts. I'd like to especially thank my Grandma Wassil who supports me and everything I do. Without her my entry to this book wouldn't be possible.

In a Blink of an Eye

Never imagined it'd come to this
I guess we never paced ourselves
So let's try to work this out
You make forgetting look like a sport
Unlike me, you never broke a sweat

Don't blink, you might miss fate's true face
But I'll never forget yours
Ignorance is sweet bliss
So this is what I get
For being your least potential
For being so forgettable
Absent-minded in a blink of an eye
Don't blink, you might miss fate's true face
The sunshine is where I'll be looking
The rules are meant to be broken
I don't care if you're taken
I'll talk to you if I want to
We both suffer from whiplash

Absent-minded in a blink of an eye

She had the same head as me last year
That let you fool me
You will not control me with fear
Your full moonlight won't outshine me

I don't care if you're taken
I'll talk to you if I want to
We both suffer from whiplash

Absent-minded in a blink of an eye

Julian Powell

Paradise

The sun was shining brightly
but gentle is its rays
The water of the lands
makes little ripples from the waves
Children laugh together
as they run and play
This isn't just one or two seasons
but each and every day
Harmony is the song
that's sung throughout the world
Love, peace, a spiritual happiness
lives within every boy and girl
Flowers shine like rainbows everywhere
Trees grow by the hundreds
producing apples, peaches, and pears
The fragrance of the flowers
trees and green grass
Spreads throughout the nations
like perfume spilling out of its glass
Wildlife becomes tame
and joins the domestic home
Life is without a care or want
and no one needs to roam
Paradise, oh paradise,
is a life that can't be best
Paradise is the life
I would like to meet

Michelle L. Berry

Rolling Hills Tour

We arrived on top of the Rolling Hills
It just seems as if time stood still
The panorama with the drama
beauty just surrender
what a wonder
it's something like to no other
It demonstrates beauty captivate
it just couldn't wait
When all is said and done
the Rolling Hills are the only one
It's beauty galore
sight-seeing and more, what a
beautiful tour
from shore to shore
you couldn't ask for more
But wait
you just can't escape
that beautiful landscape
As the beauty unfolds
I believe it's one of the wonders
of the world
Fountain Park has the highest peak
exactly one hundred twenty-eight feet
As the plane goes by
it brightens the sky
a red light is its guide
Some people go down to the water
because it makes them feel better
The tour guides are superb
the best I have seen or heard
We need more Rolling Hills Tours
I just want to say
what a beauty is Jamaica Bay

When we stopped at a certain spot
on top of Fountain Park
we could see Manhattan a lot
At Penn Park as you walk
you can see Spring Creek Tower
more beautiful than ever
On the Rolling Hills Tour
to the hills and mountain we soar
It's a beautiful sight to see,
the trees, hills, and sea
I hope and I pray
that the beauty of Jamaica Bay
will always remain this way
The Tour is a success
everyone did their best
keep on pushing and improving
it will be better and better
Before I come to the end
congratulations to all my friends
The landfill has become
the Rolling Hills by the bay
Beauty all around, so just come on down

Arnold Best

I Long for You

I long for you like whisper longs for lips,
When hazy dusk puts on the silver pining;
When wistful night delightful moonlight sips,
Matchmaking sighs and knitting shadows' binding.

Like a budded rose in bursting for a touch
Of the first beams of a tender-basking morning,
A new beginning comes from nothing much
To reach the highest decibels of longing.

I long for you like dusk for cooling breeze,
To ruse away the heat of the day's molding,
To inhale love till longing slips to kiss
Of two bright stars paused in the tense beholding.

I long for you, an ocean for the shore
In reaching up to touch its silver lining;
A boat for water at the ocean's door
Of what it meant to be by birth assigning.

Ella Yanushevskaya

Born in the former Soviet Union, Ella Yanushevskaya has begun writing poetry being a University student. She studied linguistics under the guidance of a well-known Russian poet Victor Krivulin. In 1998, she moved to the USA. In December of 2010, Eber & Wein published her poem "There is Beauty in Every Disgrace" in Sunflowers and Seashells: Days Remembered. *On April 20, 2011, PublishAmerica released her poetry book,* There is Beauty in Every Disgrace. *In November 2011, her poem "Incendiary Dance" was featured in the deluxe hardbound edition of* Stars in Our Hearts. *Her second poetry book,* The Spinning Wheel of Love, *was published on November 28, 2011.*

Hell No! (modern)

You thought that you were so hot, walkin' around like you were non-
  stop.
Professional with your game, takin' them hearts like love was cocaine.

You had your chick on the side, taken with me, but more with your
  pride.

Or did your massive ego decide you need them for show?

I thought that you were the man, but you were nothing at all.

Now you've got tears in your eyes, like you could apologize!

Hell no! You've got this woman calling up my phone,
Asking who I am, where we were, what we did!

Hell no! You're acting like she's crazy, as if she's gone…
When you're the one who did wrong!

Linda Sheffield

Can you relate? This poem was written because of the constant moral breakage in our society where there are constant situations with "the other man/woman" as well as the "victim" who is being cheated on with that person. The poem turned song "Hell No" is one of many that I wrote as Lynnaya, utilizing the inspiration that life has given to me. I have displayed other songs such as "Destitute" and "Consider Her" on the site as well. Primarily, I am a songwriter turned poet and vice versa. If you would like to see/hear those works, you are welcome to go to the link: http://music.blackplanet.com/Lynnaya/. Thank you in advance for enjoying my work!

Untitled

When I first met you,
My world skipped a beat.
The sun became the moon,
And then cold to heat.
Roses weren't red.
Violets weren't blue.
But all was okay,
Because I had you.
All of a sudden, a distance between us,
like a heart-wrenching scandal.
Trust me, I'd be lying if I said
Losing you is something I can handle…

Rebecca Williams

You're Beautiful

Different people
Different looks
Different scents
People telling you positive or negative things
Believing you're beautiful or ugly
Truth is…
Beauty is in the inside
No one knows who you really are
Or what kind of person you are
Only you can judge yourself
Who are they to tell you who or what you are?
You're beautiful
Don't let anyone tell you otherwise
True beauty is on the inside
People can't see it
Only you can see what beauty you are
God gives you your looks
No matter what, you're beautiful
Don't forget that
Never forget, you are and always will be beautiful

Lewis A. White Sr.

Dark Ones

The dark ones watching from their wall
Waiting for the humans to meet their fall
The golden sun has kept them as slaves
But as the apocalypse approaches, they dig the grave
Twilight descends, hiding the sun like a cloud
The world is covered by a silent shroud
Judgment will be passed, punishment given
The world no longer belongs to the livin'
The dark ones smile, their work is done
They are no longer afraid of the sun

Anna E. Manley

On the Edge

At a place between deepest anger,
and the most peaceful calm
Is where I've lost myself
this time.
Barefoot on the rocky ground I stand
behind me my white gown billows.

Pain and beauty go hand in hand
Love and hate keep close council

You and I we are north and south
so far away, so different
yet so close and so together.
You keep me from the cliff edge,
yet I remain on the edge of a blade.
Forever between two places
no belonging do I do.

I've begun to make a place here,
Alone and on the edge.
Then you balanced me out
by standing by my side.

Forever between two places.
Forever with you by my side.

Pennee Wilson

Think

Have you taken just a moment
Out of this busy day
To meditate with God a while
You'll find that it will pay

Just think about the blessings
That He has sent you down
Then put a smile upon your face
And wipe away that frown

For here's a bit of kindness
Please join me in a cup
When you're feeling this low down
The only way left is up

So rise above your sadness
And spread good will to all
When there's a pebble In your path
Please try hard not to fall

Rather tell yourself instead
I refuse to feel so sad
God gave me the greatest gift of all
A wonderful mother and dad.

Violet Bennin

America: Our Country

America's known as the U.S.A.
The land of plenty, we've heard them say.
She's always been called "The Land of the Free"
A blessing, being born here, for you and for me!

We're richer than others, from opportunities galore
Inviting to all peoples, from each foreign shore.
We welcome them all, to come live side by side
As the diversity and knowledge takes us forward with pride.

We've sacrificed plenty, to give others a hand,
And to give them the freedom, for which we all stand.
A chance to achieve is in all that we do;
Never giving up, is what gets us through!

We may make mistakes, and do some things wrong,
But making it right is what keeps us strong.
Our offspring inherit the lessons we've learned,
As our pages in history are forever turned.

There is birth, and then death; of this there's no doubt!
What we do in between, defines what we're about.
Our blessings come from God above, in our lives every day
His love is never-ending, even in times that we stray.

Our lives may be uncertain as we go along our way,
But faith gives us courage to face tomorrow's new day.
Who we are and what we have are all gifts from above.
God bless America, this land that I love!

Sandra M. Orem

O God, How Wonderful Thou Art

I thank you Lord for fragrant flowers and trees,
and views from mountaintops that please.

I sing your praise along the babbling brook,
and for the beauty of reflected look,
for rivers wide that with the current's flow,
and in my heart, your love I really know.

When springtime fruit trees burst into full bloom
and blossoms can be seen from every room,
I know that later in the year
the ripened fruit will once again appear.

For fields of corn that stand so straight and high,
and flying birds against a brilliant sky,
I thank you, Lord.

For farms with good rich soil,
and for the work thereon of honest toil,
for homes to raise our families so dear
the promise is that just around the bend,
we'll see God's glorious rainbow at the end.

I once again sing praises from my heart,
O God, how wonderful thou art!

Grace T. Lefever

The Cave at Lascaux 1. The Origin

Cold windswept, desolate, glaciered snows millenniums pressed
So constant wintered the tenuous course of Earth and Sun
Incessant snows that ever weighted lay a colossus of ice become
And now most calamitous spread the oblate North encrust.

Phantom forms spectral shapes sharp edged with massive wails
Of crushing weight resounding of the havoc mete rise and fall
And undulate, shatter rock, fragment trees, amass and separate
Scar and cover land and seas sculpt the tall mountain peaks.

Pale light and distant Sun deepening shadows of the void beyond
But stayed! The chilled Earth its dark course run poised
At aphelion returns restored to a warm and temperate sun
Yet environed uniquely graced a living planet fraily placed.

Dark swirling clouds of overcast strangely lit wrathlike
Of nature wrought the great ice lightning split thunders
On raging torrents that flood the land and burrow beneath
An Earth besieged by demons, by vengeful Furies seized.

Marked and fixed by seasons the Northern wastes reclaimed
Burgeoning fields and forests clear lakes and flowing streams
Life evolving in a savage continuum now manifest with creatures
Erect and brave who venture to the entrance of a cave.

Russell Landwehr

The Treasure Called Time

This precious commodity can't be bought or sold
It's not found on your statement of your portfolio
It's worth more than silver, it's worth more than gold
Worth less to the young, worth more to the old

Some take it for granted; some have an abundant supply
Some can't get enough, they're never satisfied
You can spend this commodity however you choose
When and how you spend it is up to you

You might have a dream that you want to come true
Reach for it; before it's too late, you know what to do
We think that tomorrow will always come
But today could be the last with your daughter or son

You could wake up tomorrow and ask yourself why
Your loved one is gone there were no goodbyes
So if you're working, and say, sorry, I don't have time
It's just an excuse; you should know it's a sign

That you're spending your time on things that don't matter
Instead make memories to keep and don't let them scatter
Spend your time wisely because it doesn't last
Time goes by like a flick or a flash
Tomorrow becomes today it comes so fast,
Before you know it the present and the future turn into the past

Carol A. Erikson

Arlington

Row upon row
It's all so insane
Grave markers glow
War causes lots of pain

Many have died in vain
Jones, Smith and Crow
Some had nothing to gain
Somebody, you know

Never given a chance to grow
Expendable they have been
Life, ebbs and flow
Women, as well as men

From God Almighty, Amen!

Harriet Kriner

Snowflake

I need to go see my vet Dr. Hill
He will give me a shot or a pill
I have been going there many years
I go in there barking and come out in tears
Dr. Hill will always be my friend
And will be until the end.
When I go in I see this monster cat
It's friendly, I'm glad it's not a rat
I see dogs, cats, many kinds and sizes
I bet they are in for some big surprises
When I see my master near harm
I forget my sickness and will be her alarm
When she is working in the yard
I am watching her and on guard
I warned her about a coral snake
She had time to get a hoe and rake
I will always be by her side
She knows I have always tried

Ruby V. Hyatt

He Endured It All

There was nothing special about the whipping post
Thousands were tied there at the most
There was nothing special about the cat-o-nine tails
Many suffered and many wailed
But with each stripe that was laid
It was for our healing he surveyed
He endured it all just for you, but he really didn't have to
There was nothing special about the cross
The two thieves paid the same cost
And those nails were nothing new
All who were hung had these too
As he hung there in silence
The weight of this world hung in the balance
He endured it all just for you, but he really didn't have to
He took the slurs and the spitting
For he knew they done it unwitting
All the cruelty he went through
He was not the first, this is true
But he endured it all just for you, and he really didn't have to
What was so special then?
It was his blood that was left when
Those cat tails ripped through his skin
While his blood soaked that whipping post
The soldiers laughed and boast
At which one had hurt him the most
This blood that stained that old cross
Was shed so this world would not be lost
Each precious drop was filled with love
No other can do what his blood does
And he endured it all for me and you
And it's plain to see that he simply didn't have to
But I am so glad he did, aren't you?

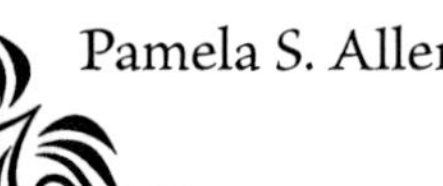

Pamela S. Allen

A Moment of Silence

I take a moment of silence...
To ponder on my blessings.
From life, to health, to thanks to God for giving me yet another day—
A day of sunshine, when there could have been rain,
A day of laughter, when there could have been tears,
A day for a home-cooked meal that was warm and not burnt,
A day of rushing from here to there,
with only the desire in my heart that I wanted to be home.
Home to rest my head with a covered roof, soft blankets
and the comfort of all I love dear resting near me.
As the sun sets and I close my eyes to yet another day,
I take a moment of silence...
To praise God for all my blessings.

Julie Armstrong

Doom's Might Clutch

Life's nothing but 'Crush'
Too much you shouldn't rush
Cruz doom's mighty clutch
Leaves no one un-touch

Each object on this Earth
Subject to death and birth
No one nevertheless
Far away from access

Yield without delay
Obey 'Him' and pray
Everything to decay
Nothing here to stay

What is birth? "God Send"
What is death? "The End"
Don't be dis-content
Seek enlightenment

High, low, big or small
Everyone's hath a fall
No one's safe and sound
Doom's broom brooming around
Don't forget mortality
Remember reality
No one's long lived here
Life's short term affair

Sooner the better
Find out the matter
Life's due to an end
Listen, don't pretend

As long as your soul
In body rock 'n' roll
You flash like spectrum
Fade and glow's conundrum

Kuldip S. Gentleman

The Veteran (our lost and forgotten heroes)

In a small town in Wisconsin, on a cold winter day,
a man sits in a bar with nothing to do or say.
As he stares out the window at the falling snow,
he sits and dreams of a better place to be or go.
He dreams of home and his wife and kids to see,
but his head is all twisted from the bad stuff he's seen.
He's been to Iraq and Afghanistan, twice in that sand,
there he lost his left eye and part of his right hand.
As he sits and thinks about what he was told to do,
it's all too much for his head to sort through.
His wife is seeing a different man every day,
his kids were told he was M.I.A.
Well there he sits with a shot and a beer,
pondering where he should go from here.
His head was so full of war and the fear of dying,
by being blown up or killed, he started crying.
He hid in a culvert until the shelling had ended,
when things were quiet he slowly ascended.
As we all know someone in the armed forces
does not run away, back down or cry.
There were the MPs with guns and hand cuffs,
they marched him away and treated him rough.
The court martial went quick, guilty as charged,
he was sent home, with a dishonorable discharge
The Washington war machine keeps rolling on,
killing or maiming our daughters and our sons.
Someone should stand up and say this is wrong,
but our fearless leaders dance to a different song.
How many times must this story be written,
each story is different each story is the same,
the only thing different are the family names.
So he sits all alone in the bar, with a lonesome stare,
his thoughts are a million miles from there.

Elmer Doerr

Owning Your Mind

I wonder if you know how precious you are to me
Laying curled up sleeping by my side
I watched as the sun rose over the window ledge
Touched a small curl of your eye lash and glittered like gold
The smell of our love was heavy in that room
The sheets were wrinkled and tossed aside
I reached down to taste your lips
And found my own body there
I wanted to reach and touch your hair
But was afraid I would awaken you
I did not want to see what was in your eyes
In that split second of waking
Would you see me or would you see her
I do not know if I still hold your mind
I have been in there for so long
I would gladly give her your body
As long as I can own your mind

Ardith L. Peoples

All Yours

You've got to help me make this heart
All for You and You alone
Because it seems like every turn
Presents some new distraction.
I gave You my all and all
I want to keep it that way.
Save me, Lord, lest I fall
And turn and go astray.
Daily dread of failure
Pulls and tugs at me.
Just give me strength
To know You're there
Even when I cannot see.
My heart, Lord, so fragile,
The temptation so strong
Like the apple in the garden
Beautiful, yet wrong.
Remind me of Your master plan
Save me, help me along.
The doubts I feel,
I wonder, "Am I good enough?"
To do this task You have for me?
The answer, no, I still need You,
I'm still Your diamond in the rough.
Until one day I find the answers
Conquer, triumph, win,
You'll welcome me with open arms
Speak, gently, "My child, come in."
Then will I see and know the truth
Behind these present trials,
Present myself, fall at Your feet
And worship for a while.

Kelsey Wells

Two-Twos (At the Party)

Hear their laughter
And then their footsteps
Soft
And then loud
Two two-year-olds
Want
To join the crowd

The crowd welcomes
Them
With cheery talks
Or an outstretched
Limb

Now the party's ended
The crowd dispenses
Oh what would I give
For a little help
How about
A pair of registered nurses

Harry M. Davidson

Violated

Violated personal space, innocence interrupted;
Deprived of dignity, a bodily assault.
Threatened and defiled,
wounds invisible to the naked eye
Tossed to the sharks, bereft,
Helpless and alone, seeking solace for my pain.

What did make him think I was easy prey?
Did I lead him on by an act or look?
No intent had I to tempt this loathsome beast.
Read about in papers, heard on the TV;
How can this be happening? Be happening to me?

Invasion of my mind, now tortured by the crime…
Expunge this vile act; dear God, please give me strength.
Tarnished sense of worth, lowly worm am I;

Not so, not so, I cry.
Bruised perhaps, but not destroyed.
Healing must begin, serenity must reign,
Peace must be restored, given time and space…
Determined to survive.

Elaine M. Uonelli

How to Enjoy a Happy Marriage and Family

Husband and wife respectively obey theirs human natures,
Aye husband and wide dignify each other and maintain holiness,
Simplicity of couple always growing happiness and equanimity,
Thereupon couple always capable to enjoy happy family.

Inflexible faith, purity and true love-most essential of couple,
Love not ever to go quit and lose the faith-love stay in last forever,
Couple holily feels-each other for welfare of marriage and family,
Its transparency always marriage and family raises happy.

Clean interrelationship capable to safe vow of the marriage,
Couple is sticking together to make marriage and family happy,
Couple belongs to habitual truthfulness for happiness of family,
Transparent love an faith can create a joyful family.

Marriage is the temple of the love, hopes and happiness,
Couple is to be "one mind" physically, mentally and practically,
Reside together, understanding each other for the equanimity,
Thereupon raises integrity and appearing happy family.

Always love and feels each other for happiness of marriage,
Think together and co-operation each other for welfare of family,
Feels each other for divine friendship to get a peaceful family life,
Consequence of it enjoys a peaceful and happy family.

Equability play an important role all over the marriage,
Aye share weal and wore to gets the marriage and family happy,
Work and think together with equanimity for enjoy happy family,
Veracity, forgive and forget helps to enjoy a happy family.

Marriage is the best custom to come over a family life,
It view aye family happiness, reside together and romanticism,
Fidelity and sanctity able to fulfill the expectations of marriage,
Strong faith and heartily love always rise up happy family.

Suresh C. Halder

The Substitute Self

I hid myself in a tower and sent a substitute
Who would do everything that they expected,
Until habit had made the tower a prison and
And in terror I struggled to be free.

Imagining freedom, I masqueraded
In a cloak of icy indifference
And would do nothing that they expected,
Until habit had made a new kind of prison
And in weakness, I wept to be free.

Weeping, I beat my fists upon locked doors
And pounded at barred windows
Seeking my freedom all to no avail,
Until in love I found the courage to be real
And then I knew love was the key.

Marilyn D. Aberle

The Art of Nature

A sudden breeze that sends my gaze upward, into
the glittering stars, gleefully accepting.
Their silent gestures allured me slowly
I ventured into those pleading lights of
dawn, and ahead the

desolate road seemed to stream in many directions,
outstretched rivers leading to darkness,
currents rolling, then dragging me under
till I vanished in a midnight painting of
a stillness that swallowed me alive,

and from below, I glimpsed the faint flickering above, and around
me green leaves began to grow—a sheltered paradise,
an invisible garden shield,
a guardian protecting me from behind
the frame of a masterpiece.

But the faceless figures of the dark wandered
with the wind, contaminating my mind in weakness
as the infectious chill spread,
stretching to reach me, like deadly phantoms—
frightening my last bit of sanity,

and then soothing comfort as
the serenity of the nighttime began pointing itself
into the fading blue sky.
I glance to admire the sparkling diamonds
embroidered in midnight wonder.

The moon's fragile glass light
emits a glimpse of a hundred hazy eyes, all
surrounding me with glaring pain as
I shiver away the weighing mist in which

the shadows before me become my own;
watercolors sway to remind me of
the luminosity that exists at night,
and the shade that I add to the
art of midnight.

Roxana C. Lazaro

Journey of the Human Spirit

It all began eighteen months ago when I discovered the most exciting, wonderful, fulfilling, and yes sometimes trying times of my life. No, I've never climbed Mt. Everest nor have I parachuted from a plane. The fact is I'm on a journey, a spiritual journey. A journey to me is a path of life yet to be taken, the doors that are open and the ones that are closed. You see not only I, but everybody on this planet is on the same quest as me. However my journey is made of hope, love, joy, truth, life everlasting, forgiveness, mercy, and grace. It is a road not to often taken and all to easily forgotten. It started before time began and continues with each individual's own quest for truth. As I watch and look all around me I am painfully aware of our enemies. They try to drag us down and suck the very life out of all who dare to give heed to it. Many people take this path only to find the darkness envelope them. And yet it is comfortable to them. Some think they have the answers to life and the journeys they are to take and yet they die. Oh beautiful, beautiful is the fire in my spirit. You see I know a truth only the spirit can touch. I know how it feels to fly on an eagle's wing and I know what it is to hide in the shadows of my soul. God alone reached down to pull me out and stand me on the rock. No one else touches that part of me, nothing else fills the gaping void that goes to the inner most part of my spirit. Into the real person, not the one you see. Oh but He is there I can feel Him, breathe Him, live for Him, so close to touch and yet I am to remain awhile longer. I look forward to my path to be taken, and yet I never look back on what's been forgiven, for how can I look back on what is no longer there? I know of the battles being waged around me and yet I am thankful for that which is not seen. To behold the spiritual world around us would strike terror in the hearts of men. And yet I move forward, continue on, knowing my steps are guided. I have an invisible shield, red in color and yet white as snow. My eyes have seen the face of evil, my heart has felt the darkest of black. My soul has walked the fence line only to be tossed by the wind.

Then I saw His hand extended as if to hold tight, without letting go.
He puts me on the road leading up, my heart sings, my soul praises
His name for I have found peace and restoration. For that which was
asleep has been awakened within me. I know not how long I will be on
this journey, it matters not. It is but my heart's desire to live each day
to please Him.

Darcie Ciesielski

Upper Rogue River Valley

A cobalt sky, white puffy clouds floating over the green of the
mountains.
Evergreen trees reach majestically toward the heavens. Alongside
the winding road grows wild blackberries and mustang grapes. In the
country of the Upper Rogue River valley.

The river beginning in the Cascades on the way to the sea, sometimes
it floats lazily and serene past the willows and shrubs. Other places it
is rough, wild like the rogue that it is. Rapids and falls showing how
powerful this river of the Upper Rogue River Valley can be.

In the wilds of the backcountry where there are hunting, fishing,
camping and backpacking in the woods everything is free. Being one
with nature, deer, elk and bear are what you hope to see. It is easy to
see all the wonders that God made in this beautiful Upper Rogue River
valley.

Donna Tumey

We Walk Together

If you be in Texas
And I be in Maine,
We walk together.
If you be enlightened
And I be insane,
We walk together.
If you be the Savior of the world we live in,
And I be the expression of error and sin;
If you carry the torch for compassion and love,
And I wield the dagger that murders the dove;
If your eyes are clear and mine clouded by doubt;
Your path straight and even, but I know no way out
Of the suffering and fear that torment my heart,
We still walk together, we can't walk apart
For we are one.
If you be deceased, and I remain,
We walk together.

Karen Dalin

Move Forward with Courage

Move forward with courage in your heart
Break out of your mold and be unique
Let God take command over your life
And listen closely as the Holy Spirit speaks.
There will be times when you must take action
For at the core of one's faith, they need commitment,
And to procrastinate or to delay can be fatal
Being guided by complete faith brings peace and contentment.
Chart a new course for yourself and move forward
And don't let yourself be bogged down with all kinds of fears
Always remember that God is there to help you succeed,
For it takes determination to leave the nest
And to hold back the tears.
Move ahead with courage towards your dream,
For God's promise of an abundant and eternal life
Is offered to those who dare to walk the walk of faith,
So walk that path with God and lay at His feet
Your stress and strife.
Dare to dream the most wonderful dreams
Make your dreams come true by believing God will guide you
Positive dreams become realities when joined
With work faith, and trust,
For He knows your heart and your success
Become an absolute must.
My faith is based on my past experiences
And on the power and grace of God in my life
And I know having a solid faith above all else
And time set aside with God each day will eliminate strife.

Rachael Johnson

A Void Between Us

The voice came so softly,
Like the sound of softly falling snow.
It whispered, please listen carefully,
There is something you need to know.
I have never left you,
I am always close at hand.
Every time you speak to me,
I hear and understand.
There is just a veil between us.
I give you strength every day.
I listen very carefully
To all you have to say.
So keep on serving me faithfully,
Take time to kneel and pray.
Soon that veil will open
When I bring you home to stay.

Mary G. Bognar

Life's Continuing Book

When I look back over time gone by,
Months and years, my, how they fly!
It seems like yesterday the kids were young,
Full of dreams and screams, just having fun.
Now they're grown and married with kids,
Only God knows what each life bids.
We love our grandchildren, all nine the same,
But only one boy will carry on the name.
We listen and smile as they relay their dreams,
How wonderful and glorious it all seems.
Visions of our own dreams come back into view
As the gift of grandchildren made all things new.
So put your shoulder to the plow and never look back,
For those who do will always know lack.
God has a plan, just seek it and know
That you'll always be blessed wherever you go!

Beverly J. Mork

My God

I have never heard my God complain
Nor say I can't because I am too busy now.
No matter if it be worry, sadness, or pain
He always seems to find the time for me somehow.
My God is always ready to speak to me
He is always on my side.
Anytime or anywhere I happen to be
He hears my every prayer and need.
No matter what the problem, on Him, I can rely
If only I will open up my heart and hear.
He never fails to give me a reply
Always soothing my sadness and fears.
Now in return, what gift have I to give?
Perhaps somewhere along the way
Help someone a better life to live
Showing love and kindness day by day.

Geraldine Hatcher

Right Here

I visit her and hold her hand
Work-worn and wrinkly, next to her I stand
We decide to go and at the beach we walk
And with all the time passed, it's time to talk
The heartache brought on by one
The stories of how I never won
The pain of unexplained loss in life
The fear of craving a stab from a knife
The way my hands now shake
The feeling that anyone can what I have, take
It spills like water from a glass broken
Each story its own individual token
She takes them all and holds them tight
And helps me see a future clear and bright
And through this gift she gives to me
I see that far from me, she'll never be

Noemi Arana

Mantra of the Iconoclast

I am still discovering who I am
And I have only one lifetime to do it
Nature and nurture will not shape me
I determine my own identity
I blaze my own trail
My actions are my own
My thoughts are my own
My writing is my own
Society does not impress me
Nor does conformity
People don't use their minds anymore
Neglecting the grain of salt
Making common sense a rarity
Tuning out of reality
We live in an intellectual tragedy
Where the rebel is ridiculed
The individual is oppressed
Revolutionaries are silenced
Renegades and intellectuals are ignored
And the mind is neglected
Seeds sown in schoolyard cliques
Sprouting into society
Taking full bloom in the government
Propaganda, indoctrination, suppression
The shackling of another generation
Where is our hope? Our freedom?
The majority are useless
Freedom-change rely on
The iconoclast

Jessica Anderson

The Dancer Within

When we are lost in a moment of despair dance.
Most of us have that dancer within.

Let go of the stress jump up and down. A child's tantrum is a dance.
A quick step into a new job fresh out of college a dance.

Why can't you be as excited when you're taking a slightly
shorter step out of retirement.

How about when you fall in love.
You dance to get ready for those first few dates.
You give that little jump when you're having your first baby.
That first dog or cat that picks you to care for them together.

That dance has to be you when your partner can't dance on their own.
I know that it's hard yet you must keep dancing then.

And when your partner or you are dying don't lose that dance.
It would be easier to create an angel.
Help them thru to be a powerful spirit for those who follow.

I can dance when I follow, I can dance when I lose myself.
If I stop dancing remind me that my life is a dance.

Remind me I must learn the steps and change the steps.
We must flow with all the spirals that entertain our life.

Will you dance with me?

Ann Wahl

They're the Flower and I'm the Stem

Every day I fear going to school
Because the kids don't think I'm cool
They approach me with a smirk
Then push me up to the lockers, calling me a jerk
They say this because I'm not as popular as them
They think they're the flower and I'm the stem
I come to school not knowing what's next
Before I know it, I have a new text
Of course it's something mean and cruel
It reads: nobody likes you, you ugly fat fool
That's not it, there's more to come
The bullying has just begun . . .
Bullying is a problem worldwide
Many people have tried and tried
It must end already
Because it makes many unsteady
I'm not a victim but I've seen it occur
And I'm sure those people wish it was a blur
It comes to a point after running and hiding
That they even approach dying
Forms of bullying have progressed over time
Now it's even online
We must stop this trend
And bring it to an end!

Nicki Meckler

Freak Show

They call me a freak and say I'm mad
they say it's wrong, too bad
I'm a freak show it's all I am
I'm just another wanna be
Yeah I'm a freak show that's what I'm meant to be
black eyes and nails of red
all I am is a worshiper of the dead
I'm an animal and wrong in the head
they say I need to go
I'm a freak show
that's all I am
I'm a freak show and that's who I be
I'm a freak show and just a nobody
I'm just a freak show they will get what they get
because I may be a freak show
but I'm not ashamed of it
Yeah I'm strange and I look it too
but I don't even care
they don't get
I'm more than a freak show

Warren Watts

We Are Birds

We are birds,
Ready to fly.
Yet here we stand, in herds,
Beneath the sky.

We have wings,
To spread out and soar.
Yet, to the ground we cling.
We walk and run, but nothing more.

Why do we stay,
Held down this way?
So full of fear.
But freedom is near.

We are in a cage.
We are birds behind bars.
Too afraid to turn the page;
We never go far.

We, ourselves, stay inside.
We keep our wings down.
With a smile, we gaze outside.
Inside we frown.

Why don't we fly
Into the beautiful blue sky?
Why do we fill ourselves with fear?
We are birds; freedom is here.

Patricia Arena

Stories

I've seen my children grow
from young to old
they've heard my stories
they have heard my tales

As a young kid I have watched
people as they grow
I've seen the world above and below
families die and families grow

My time is short for I must go
back to my own little world
where the trees are green
the breeze is clean
and I hold my family close to me

My tales are done
my stories have gone
my memory fails me so
I'm at a loss
for I want to watch my family's children grow

Mary Laclair

You Are...

You are my light guiding me through dark, troubled times
You are my hope when I'm giving up to carry on
You are my protector of love and light when I'm scared
You are my everything forever and always
You are mine
I never learned until now just how much I love you
I never want this to end
I never want us to hurt each other
I love you with all my heart and soul
You mean life or death to me
You are more than my world
You are a beautiful end in a wonderful life
You will be mine forever
We will love each other forever and beyond
I want my last memories to be with you
My last words spoken to you
My last sight to be your beautiful face
I want you forever
I love you and always will

Becca Straw

Labyrinth

Taken to the light where all answers are found,
Walking the night in gloom, ghosts all fly around.
Haunt me in this black dimension's haze
This heart is torn apart by desire's frozen blade.

Lost my way in paths of stone.
Seek the light questions beneath me.
Propel the journey, leaving string below.
Guide the maze for what I believe.

Unholy place that hungers the lost
Specters undead speak through words of frost.
In canyons unknown, searching for your loft,
The lanterns ahead leave back the cross.

Spirit that shines from the walls,
Save me from the shades that crawl.
Show me where to kill the minotaur.
Test us for what we really are.

Too much at stake to fall behind,
Spawn of Taurus on our heels.
Walls crash and crumble as we run
We will die before we kneel.

The end is not in sight.
Take away the throne of Minos.
Eyes will fade to gray
And the walls will fall.

Devyn Shibla

Recoil & Ricochet

Contemplation of words forgotten
Two fingers resting on the bridge of my nose
Crumbled paper filling my waste basket
Hesitant to compile these nouns and verbs to life
Worried that these words may falter

As I embrace this pen even harder—
The words sit there as if in limbo state
 As I try and regurgitate a complete thought
Without the connection of verbiage expression

Lines finally formed, paragraphs finally built
My heart seeps on to the sheet and blossoms meaning
Erected to the masses, eyes imbibe the words, and form opinions
 Impressions ricochet back to my doorstep, negative and positive results
Confuting emotions arise: criticism disturbs my core

Dedicated to the cause of definition
Infinite ideas demand to be echoed through the ink of my pen
My thoughts beseech me to continue my craft
So these pages shall always give life, knowledge, emotion, depth,
and meaning to writers everywhere

Lekeya Mosley

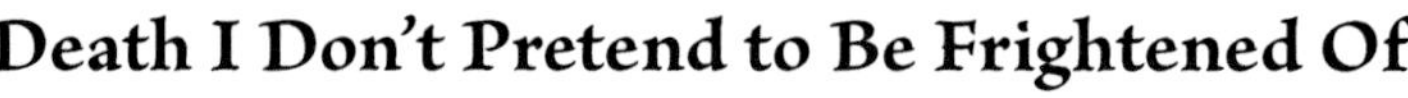

Death I Don't Pretend to Be Frightened Of

Death I don't pretend to be frightened of.
I was the six year old given ten years to live with
The snake waiting at her foot and the promise of
No pain before that but a price of some salvation I doubt
I even knew the meaning of before it was caught
In the dream of a white-blazed garden
And the golden-haired child and this feeling of warmth
I was so sure would ease out my soul
As easy as a man pulling out a blade of grass
If not for something I had been given and had taken.

Death I don't pretend to be frightened of.
I was the girl of two passages of seven years
With sixty-six weights pulling on wrists
To be opened in a flourish of self-denial and desperation
Yet to be written in verse of my own,
That sad psalm that found itself within all those other
Beautiful women of history who cast their words to the ground
And then their tired spirits to the sky.

Death I don't intend to be frightened of.
I will greet him as a friend and a confidant,
Grasp his hands inside my own and
Say quietly of the woman resting between my shoulder blades
Who called for him once or twice or maybe so many times
That the stars would lose track.
I will smile simply, showing not sorrow nor happiness
But only the human path I carved
When I finally forgot about searching for him.
I will meet him not pleading for any more time
But only asking to be taken quickly, Without fuss,
Merely with the leftover message to loved ones not to grieve
After all, I could have left earlier. I could have left no words.

Remember I was never frightened to leave the life I was given
But he was determined I would at least be thankful to have had it at all.

Ciera Durden

Love Ya!

When I sleep, I dream of you.
I melt away and dream of you.
Sometimes I don't know if it's a mirage
but I always see your face and I hear your voice inside my head,
because
I'm missing you so much.
You take my breath away, every minute you're gone.
My world is empty,
no matter what I do without you here.
Baby you have shaken all of my existence.
When I'm with you baby,
bliss is all I have come to know.
Your heart and arms are all I have come to know,
they're my comfort; they're my world of peace.
I'm running, I didn't see you coming.
Blinded it's all so stunning.
I never want to let you go.
I always hear angels sing
when you call out my name.
I hear a thousand doves
sing when you call my name.
Baby your love changed everything for me.
The chemistry is all blinding,
it makes me feel so amazing
but it feels like something so much more.
You make my pain stop.
You make the beat of my heart drop.
You make my heart beat right.
I can't breathe when you leave me.
I'm in love with you and don't know what to do.
Yes I love you because you always put
my love on top and put me first always.
You make my world spin with love.
Love ya!

Cache Orr

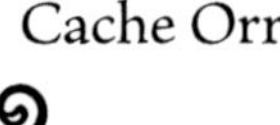

Life as I Know It

There are good and bad days.
It's your choice which one you want it to be.
We all have choices,
But the question is "Did you pick the right one?"
Don't let people pressure you.
Be yourself and not who people want you to be.
Even when times get rough battle through it.
Even if you don't succeed,
There will always be hope.
In the end never give up.

Jake Morgan

Ashes to Ashes

A space within a space,
the radiating heat glows in a cloud of red dusk
around the edges of your senses,
wavering, strengthening, building, spent;
there's a merry window made of glass,
where you can watch the goings-on of this inner world.
The window is clear and shows the crumbling of an empire, gone to
    ash.
The dead realm is raked, shoveled and tossed to the wind.
The world folds it back unto itself, welcoming.
It lights on a tree whose leaves are lost,
deep within cold winter's spell.
It floats to the sky with its brethren,
tasting the last wisps of life,
it tumbles slowly, perpetually,
back down to earth in its misery,
knowing it will one day return to frolic among its fellow trees,
dancing in the windblown fields of spring,
united once again.

Sarah Martin

If I Could Fly!

I wish the wind could carry me
So I could be next to you,
I will be the echo of the wind
saying, I love you, my man!

You knew how to surprise me
and tell me all the beautiful things,
Now, you pretend not to remember
not even saying good morning or a kiss.

I guess you must start all over again,
and don't you forget, my man!
If you hear the echo from the wind,
it's just me saying, I love you, man!

Martha Velazquez

Struggle

My home is on the streets,
I need
food,
love,
and
warmth.
I lay on the cold ground wondering if I'll see tomorrow.
Will my life ever be normal again?
Will I ever find my true love?
Will I ever start a beautiful family?
Will I ever get a job?
I try God, I try.
I try to survive, that's my main struggle.

Kelly Reed

It's Her

There are times that I wish I could quit
And walk away from it all
Throw my hands in the air
But then I get that call

Her voice is nothing special
Neither too mean or too sweet
But it's what I live for
When I am facing uncertain defeat

There's times when I lay awake thinking
About my future with her
Will it last for eternity?
As for that I'm not sure

Sometimes I sit and stare
She fidgets and fusses and makes unusual stirs
What she doesn't know
Is that I am not looking for wrongs
I'm just wondering how long I will be hers

How long will I be what she wants in her life?
How long will I be in her mind?
How long will she live with my faults and my wrongs?
And will she realize that I am not her kind

I hope she knows how much I love her
I hope she knows nothing will ever change that
I hope she knows that I worship the ground she walks on
I hope she knows I even worship that cat!

Darcie Emerson

Hayley Williams

I was born for this
And so was she
Let the flames begin
Like her hair, obviously

crushcrushcrush
I've got one on her
The only exception
She's who I prefer

The pressure is gone
When I watch her perform
Hallelujah I found her
It's a miracle, I'm sure

She's all I wanted
Though we've never met
My world shines brighter
How's she so perfect?

My misery business
Went away with a whoa
When I crossed the fences and ignorance
To the promise land of Paramore

I feel no emergency
Things are finally looking up
No more conspiracy
I'll never let this go

So here we go again
It's our life, it's all we know
That's what you get
When you fall for Paramore

Justin VanDuren

Wondering

we run, we walk, we skip and hop to the beat of some unknown drum!
One wonders if by chance we stop, to contemplate the lot.
That place of our hearts! What we have done, what we are doing?
The reasons for! All the reason more to breathe, to smell, to touch,
to hear that beat of that heart that steers.
That factor, that so compels in us all, the tension and the fear.

Joseph Demicco

Eternity

I believe in my heart,
We shall never be far apart.
There is a place where I will wait,
I know you won't be late.
When God calls us to be near,
Neither one of us will have fear.
United once again,
I will greet you with a grin.
There is no need to hurry,
I don't want you to worry.
I will always be close by,
You will feel me, if you try.
We are meant to be together.
I will love you forever.

Sami Siegel

Love Song Gone Wrong

Once Love stood tall,
strong and brave and true.
Love was promised forever,
nothing could rip her apart.
Love stood beautiful,
Love was pure and sure.
But Love was blind,
and so Love was hurt.
Love was broken,
and then Love bled.
Love was beautiful,
now Love is dead.
So Love was burned,
and now Love hides.
Love is disguised,
sits in a corner as she cries.
Listen close for Love's sad moan,
a hurt too great for even Love to atone.

Darby Casperson

Andella's Girl

Everybody knows Adella's Girl
They've known her through the years
Somewhat witty and amusing
But she'll tell it like it is.

She says she's got folks figured out
How they'll try to keep you guessing
They'll throw a curve and hide their hand
And try to take away your blessing

Beware of dogs, hook'em up
Don't let them out your sight
'Cause Andella's Girl knows this for sure
They're just not about what's right.

Mutt or purebred
They'll throw you under a bus
Andella's Girl knows this for sure
Some dogs you just can't trust.

Emma Johnson

Fall

All the leaves' color change
Air is crisp and never strange
Today, today the start of fall
Full of joy and wonder for all
Time for the magic to finally come
Festivals and Halloween are only some
Little kids play and shout
As tiny leaves dance about
Warm nights and sunny days
My only wish that fall stays
Farmers soon harvest their crop
The lovely days never stop
Dead leaves bringing cheer
Little children laughter we hear
Sadness quickly leaves the mind
The smell of candy corn we find
Dead leaves dance to the ground
A sign fall is here without a sound.

Emily Creed

Soft Murmurs

Soft murmurs are heard as the wind blows so free
and touches the leaves of each swaying tree.
Moments of bliss as the leaves sing their praise,
to the coming of light to each bright new day.
Soon leaves will fall to cushion the sound,
of God's forest creatures as they wander around.
Now snow softly falls as winter is here,
to cover the leaves at the close of the year.
Next Spring shall return and a new cycle begins,
when soft murmurs are heard and the wind blows so free,
and touches new leaves of each swaying tree.

Lorna F. Rawn

The Stranger

He extended His hand to help carry my load, I said no, I could do it
    alone;
it just could be re-balanced when needed. Dark clouds were forming;
the breeze was now a strong wind. The stranger drew closer, but I
didn't need anyone's help. I was determined I could carry this load
on my own! I trudged on, but the load was heavier. I tried to shift the
weight, but it didn't budge. Heavy rains started and the path became
a muddy, slippery mess! Suddenly, the sides collapsed. Now, it became
wider and deeper. Each step became harder than the one before. I
began sinking in the muddy water. I screamed for help, but no one
answered. Where did everyone go? Hot tears mixed with sweat ran
down my cheeks. I couldn't hold on to the load anymore. My knees
began to buckle, I was sinking, and I just didn't care anymore! I did
something that hadn't been done in years, I humbly prayed for the man
who wanted to help to return. Amazing! I shifted the load. Rising to
my knees, slowly, I stood! One step, then another through the rising
water, then more! Why wasn't the load so heavy anymore? I looked up;
there was the stranger. His face looked familiar. I heard Him call, but
ignored Him for years; it was my Lord and Savior, not a stranger at all!

Eleanor Lake

Is It Still a Joke?

In this corner I weep
Blue eyes turned red
Wishing for that endless sleep
Even though I already feel dead
You said it was just a jest
A way for your ego to be stroked
Have you finished with your quest?
Is it still a joke?

In this place I'm stuck
Beaten from all sides I cower
No I'm not just down on my luck
The pain is a constant shower
Your smile a twist of hate
Sometimes I wish I could croak
Saying sorry is too little too late
Is it still a joke?

The scars on my arms
Tell story after story
Your whit and your charms
You flaunt your glory
But what is it all worth
When agony I wear like a cloak
The blade against skin like a rebirth
Is it still a joke?

Look deep in my eyes
You'll be haunted the rest of your life
I've heard all the lies
You killed me with my own knife
Lying on this cold tile
My mind, will, and heart you broke
Yet you won't even have to stand trial
Is it still a joke?

Danielle DeLoof

The Skies Are Leaking, and So Am I

The skies are leaking, and so am I.
But they are nothing compared to my eye.
My eyes are flowing like the rain.
But unlike the rain, my drops are pain.
Pain of things I never said or did.
Pain of knowing how I would feel if I never did.
I know now that life is short but oh so sweet.
Full of people who are a joy to meet.
I met the most perfect angel from the sky.
With voice so pure and sweet it makes me cry.
Knowing you is great, but knowing you are my friend,
Keeps me going because now I know how I will end.
Living my life with my special pea in a pod.
You make me seem all the more odd.
Your laugh, oh how I love to hear it.
Knowing I was the cause of it.
I can't express how much you mean to me.
Because in truth you are inside me.
You know what to say to make me feel alright.
When I'm sad you never let me leave your sight,
Until I smile and say I'm alright.
But the truth is you make me feel alright.
Like the most perfect man ever made.
But the truth, you are the most perfect maid.
Angel with a heart so big, and a voice so sweet.
An angel like you I will never meet
My love, my heart and my guardian angel.

Joshua LaCount

Where Have You Gone, Moon?

Dear luminous moon, where are you this hazy night?
For the hours of darkness seem dimmer without your soft light
You've concealed yourself from the sun's unblemished rays
Refusing to reflect its beauty, declining to display
Alas, even the dullest of stars outshine you in the sky
And the clouds encasing your magnificence begin to multiply
As a soft drizzle from the billows does come,
The rain pounding the ground with a gentle hum
I tilt my head back to feel the showering rain on my face
To discover you've come back and recovered your place
Shining so brilliant and vivid in the atmosphere
Promising to not shortly again disappear
And I welcome you back with open arms, dear moon
Simply hoping you will not leave anytime soon

Samantha Vides

Proofreading in Tights: A Villanelle

The act of proofing's often Kafkaesque
O'erreanding the same page ad infinitum
Your mind longs for the mental arabesque

Your legs go numb while sitting at your desk
Inserting comma, space ad nausea
The act of proofing's often Kafkaesque

You'd like to tap dance on their driver's disk
Whilst outfitted in dresses ante bellum
Your mind longs for the mental arabesque

You've been enclosed inside an airless casque
And interred in a corp'rate mausoleum
The act of proofing's often Kafkaesque

You realize screaming "f*** you"s such a risk
You wait for a Divine inter dictum
Your mind longs for the mental arabesque

You could be home concocting lobster bisque
And fantasies keep gathering momentum
And acts of proofing are so Kafkaesque
Your solace is the mental arabesque

Gerit Quealy

Life

Appreciate love,
Appreciate hate.
You were put here for a reason,
No debate.
Don't sit around and waste away the life that's meant to live.
When the moment's right you best stand up,
Smile, and forgive.
Keep your head up, soldier,
March along the road called life.
Don't be too offended by the ones who pull the knife,
And put it in your back,
The ones who give you crap.
You're too good for that and you know too well that's a fact.
Yeah, life can suck sometimes,
But you have to walk the line, you're fine.
And never run obstacles for the people acting blind.
And when it comes down to it,
You're better off lonely
People will backstab you faster than your finding they're phony.
But look, champ,
You gotta run the race to win.
Blood, sweat, and tears,
It'll be worth it in the end.
Life's too good to waste,
You got to finish what you started,
Don't sit back and let the people think you were outsmarted.

Courtney Miszczak

Colorless

Everything I see is gray;
Everything I feel is fray.
All my world is drained of color;
My life just keeps growing smaller.

The green leaves are now bleak;
The trees important are meek.
A flower's scent is never noticed;
No color shows, not even from lotus.

The sun's gleam is but only white;
No special shine; not exceptional light.
The moon as well acts the same;
Nothing ever differs, what a hateful shame.

The water in the ocean only looks like a gray abyss,
As the sea creatures swim, not knowing they live in bliss.
All the animals hidden by all of nature's dull curtain,
To never be seen by anyone, that was made certain.

Myself is but a dark lifeless body with a pale face and a black heart;
I can't stay attached to this world or anyone, for we quickly drift apart.
All my hopes and dreams are now trapped by the colorless fears,
Torn away by the ruin of faith leaving my eyes in salty tears.

The color has faded;
We all have cried.
The world was raided;
No longer is it dyed.

Joseph Eldridge

Anybody

A time filled with wondering, being lost in her own head of a world
she's made for both to belong
call their own for those special moments
The moments of conversing that are innocent but she amounts it all
To want, a need—can this all be done for? A bond that can be broken?
No this is to last forever right?
Is that what all the fairy tales in life tell us? A connection that is fate,
destiny,
no
a magical moment.
That's what life is right? Those little moments we encounter,
She has those moments of purity, bliss, magic with him. A world of
their own, like the forest of their own from Snow White or a glass
slipper that's a perfect fit.
Dancing around her room in a state of mind that this is how life is to be
not challenged with each others ideas or making the other grow, this is
what it should be?
Was life to be made happy?
This world just for two that they make together. A desire everyone has
but what about him? She's created a world for them to belong.
A blissful, calm place of peace.
In a moment of vulnerability she shares with him this world that
belongs to just the two of them, a smile of innocence with a twinkle in
her eye, she goes to hold his hand but he draws back turns his back and
says he doesn't need anybody and walks away.

Rebecca Dolan

Shoes I'll Never Wear

Pink ballerina slippers quite uninvited, find
Their way, tiptoeing, to my heart and dance into my mind.

With tempting grace, they whisper with ribbons trailed behind,
They tickle my emotions like kisses of butterflies.

They toy with me with their, alluring twist and twirl,
Which, by my own design suggest that I could be that girl…

But no! I shut my ears against their Siren song.
As much as I'd like to believe, I know, deep down, they're wrong.

"Your rent is overdue, this stage, you do not own,"
I try to say, but they remain. They make themselves at home.

Frustrated, I pursue; but in my strain to fight them,
They overpower me, for I do find delight in them.

They really are quite lovely, and knowing so, they dance.
With scornful laughter, draw my gaze, and hold me in a trance.

I try to hide my feelings, but transparent is my skin.
They know I don't want them to go, and so, of course, they win.

I try hard to rebel by covering my eyes.
They call for just one little peek - but no. I know they lie.

"Enough!" I shout at last, and in the dark they flee.
And for a brief intermission I feel as though I'm free.

But no. Out from the curtain they bound in charming style
Catching me off guard and, yes, wringing from me a smile.

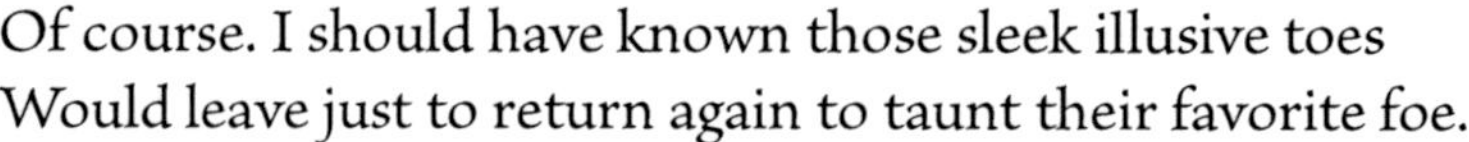

Of course. I should have known those sleek illusive toes
Would leave just to return again to taunt their favorite foe.

"Why don't you entertain me by giving me a glance,
So I can entertain you?" They sing while quick, they prance.

But fight I know I must, for though I often dare
To dream of dancing on that stage, they're shoes I'll never wear…

So why burden myself, and pay the price to see
So fine a show and witness joys for me will never be?

But so finely composed is this splendid illusion
It weaves in me unwanted hope that welcomes the intrusion.

Finally I face the fact. I know I cannot win.
For after every curtain call a new show will begin.

So now, today, I watch them, quite captivated still,
Thinking, "maybe I can dance…" but no. I never will.

Rebecca Loomis

Night

The sun sinks behind the horizon,
Casting pale shadows upon my sleepy eyes.
The light slowly withers away,
And just when I think that the darkness has come,
the moon makes its ghastly appearance.
Glowing, it banishes the darkness
And replaces it with a warm light.
Then along with it come the stars.
Little children playing in the sky,
Smiling and making the night be forgotten.

Kristin Kavaldjiev

Poetry means a lot to me. When I am having a bad day, writing about the particular event in any type of poetry helps me calm down. I live with my family (mom, dad, and brother) in San Jose. I go to Union Middle School, and I'm in the seventh grade. My hobbies include ballet, hanging around outside, and of course writing poetry.

Life

looks could be deceiving
interests can be intriguing
but the message I am receiving
should be the same that you are reading

intricate complications
that lead to early revelations
producing distinct relations
connecting our own affection

that make experiences a thing of the past
distributing memories that never seem to last
remembering upon a life I lived far too fast
yet I always remember to forget what I did last

so I let these gifts introduce the present
as I endure to preserve your presence
letting you capture the abstraction of my essence
indulging our sinister ways to dilute benevolence

now allow me to perceive predictions of the future
descending deeper in time and space to capture
our obscenities to be knowing as everyday composure
leading closer to our grave but we'll let time
finish our exposure

Luis Mendez

two miles down

beneath the north Atlantic
lies the ship of infamy
grand lady so constructed
thought none even god
himself could not
send her below the waves
the mighty power man's machine
grandest creation to set sail
would be remembered
but not for her design
rather for the cold april night
and the berg that lay in wait
floating amid the waves of the dark mysterious sea
it ripped her hull as if paper made her
from cries of despair and hopeful prayer
the event heroes and cowards did create
tapping a carpathia cpd echoes in the night
musicians play to comfort
the simple melodic prayer
and kept on as lights dim
as she went down
with groan and snap and scream
then came the silence
only the slapping of waves
for in hours thrice
gone was she
1500 souls with her
only 700 would live to tell
to recall the terror
to wonder why they were left
as it lay two miles down
a metallic grave
of sorrow and majesty

Betty A. Taucher

Hello, Who Are You?

As a child, you were like an imaginary friend
I would speak, you would answer
Along the path in life, you led
There were many times I did not listen
You loved me anyways
Hello, who are you?
You taught me to be secure in you
I have walked, leaned upon your strength
When those I loved, died, you were there
At times I shook my fist at you
Not knowing why life had to be so cruel
But you comforted me in all my grief
Searching for you I am a child, again
Hello, who are you?
Your loving kindness seeks me
I run, trying to forget you
In laughter, you find me
Sweet songs pour from my belly
How can I resist your luminous temptation?
We ride the carefree winds together
We create a pious atmosphere in unity
Hello, who are you?
Will I love you forever?
Will my heart stand before you?
Yes, I know who you are
The one and only
Beloved, by your Father
Coming face to face on an unknown day
Taking me away, I will find relief
Then together we will travel
Hello, who are you?
Jesus

Lorraine Galipeau-Watson

That Mask

Some acquaintances
Leave a mark in your
Heart forever to stay.
Their presence in your life
Now is rare; but the memory
Brings about a smile, a frown,
Or merely a tear.
There is no regret
The heartbreak will mend
The sadness will end
The experience attained
As bad as it may be
One thing was gained
There is a new friend.
Acquaintances come and go,
But that mark has taken its
Hold. It leaves you with a smile,
A frown, or merely a tear
For one knows the presence
Of that friend more than likely
Might be no more.

Frances Saiz

The Wonder of God's Love

Oh Lord, I pray take away this sorrow.
That I might find joy in You for my tomorrow.
Take the depression and the tears,
Turn them into wondrous joy and cheers.
For I know in You there is always hope
And you alone are the One who will help me cope.
O Lord, this day let Your presence sustain me.
Open my heart and understanding that I might clearly see,
The wonder of Your love for me.

Jeannie H. Gladson

Speaking of Love

When they speak of love
I think of you and my
Broken heart and wounded
Soul.

As my tears run down my face
And land on top of my chest
The pain becomes unbearable.

When they speak of love
In front of you

Do you think of me?
I don't know!
How do you feel?

Maria M. Diaz

A Gift from God

A child is a beautiful treasure from God.
A gift of love to hold, their smile fills your heart with peace,
their laughter brings joy to your soul.
Their cries wrench your heart, and you feel their pain,
but their joy brings newness to life again.
As you watch them grow and you give them to God
sometimes you don't know what to do.
You watch as they go their own way
and seek their own thing to do.
You watch as they learn, as they discover and change,
and you pray God will keep them from sin.
You pray for their protection on the path they choose to trod.
You pray when all their searching ends,
their journey will lead to God!

Mary J. Reffalt

The Old Dog

He was walking his dog
His dog was walking him
Both leashed together
To get home together
Same home, same time
A fifteen-year routine.

Both stumbled up the curb
Recovering with a happy step
Atop unsteady legs
Shuffling off toward home
Loving the togetherness
Toward the end of their journey.

I gave them space accorded to the elderly
Respect for the stumbling, honoring the longevity
Of the two old friends stumbling home together.

The old dog was limping
Accustomed to the slowing gait
Patience a long ago virtue gained
With the shuffling of the old man
Both in sync with each step
Knowing the cadence of their ages.

I loved their loving movements
Looking at each other with great fondness
Knowing the memories of the long-ago
Living the freshness of their current now
Both looking toward the end of the road
Waiting for the home around the bend.

I heard they reached home safely
Resting on the porch swing
Paw in hand, side by side
Saying goodbye in their last breaths
Grateful for the shuffling together
Making it home together just in time
One last time, together.

Roger A. Desmarais

Rain

Rain makes things beautiful
if one only takes a look
When it rains, I take a walk
down by a little brook
Rain takes care of my flowers
Rain makes my garden grow
When its cold
rain can turn into snow
When it rains the little frogs
go dancing in the street
I hope they make it safely back
before their fate they meet

Billie S. Hudson

Rimbaud in Cyprus

An unresolved solitude presses
Hot upon unquenchable thirsts
As a solitary figure walks atop quarried cliffs
      hesitates
Glances toward the beckoning Mediterranean.
Suddenly, a knife-edged remembrance
Opens the intractable wound
(Self-inflicted in Paris barely six years past)
To re-expose the irreconcilable self-deceptions vital
To the inconclusive course
Upon an inexplicable quest.
Pourquoi done existons-nous?
Je ne resterai pas longtemps ici.
1879

Ron Matros

Linger a Little While

As the sands of life slip away from our loved one,
we often ask the spirit that gave her life that she may linger a while
longer.
Linger a little while so once more the feeling of the soft firm hand can
be experienced.
Linger a little while so once more we can feel the sweet soft touch of
the lips.
Linger a little while so once more we can sense the unspoken words
from the beautiful eyes.
Linger a little while so once more we can have the feeling of oneness in
a warm hug.
Why at the end of life, which we know is coming, do we ask for more
time?
Why don't we linger for a moment now and appreciate the moments
we have before the end comes?
We busy ourselves in life without taking a moment to appreciate the
little things until the end comes, and then we look for the touch of the
hand, the lips meeting, the meeting of the eyes, and the warm firm hug.
But fret not because the spirit of God who gave us life has given us the
ability to dream and to remember. So we sit now and remember the
little things that seem to mean so much to us as the sand of life slips
away.
Ask not for a lingering moment at the end, but ask the spirit of life
to awaken in us the desire to linger a moment now and take in all the
beauty of our family and all of God's given gifts.

Julian R. Plaster

His Family

We are God's children
We are His family
He is the one who created us.
He knew we weren't perfect
Through it all, He still loves us

Some of us have turned away from His love.
Never wanting to come back
We know that we have hurt our father
We are scared to return to His love.
We know that He is waiting for us
With open arms to welcome us home
His love for us will never end.

Nothing in this world will ever measure up to
how deep His love is for us.
He loves us through our good times
He loves us through our bad times
He will never stop loving us,
even when we have stopped loving Him,
because we are His family.

Anna L Morrison

Grocery Shopping

Lights a flickering, it's time to shop.
Where's the coupons?
O Lord, help me find a flyer.
Peanut butter is now two for four dollars,
Look out.   Grey hairs are driving disabled carts.
No more left, I'll get some strawberry jam.
Hamburger sizzles, as begging hands appear.
Reduce it! Chants sound like the doxology:
Reduce it! Reduce it!
A shopper tumbles over into the pork chops.
Save him! Please save him! He's my husband.
Extricated from the pork chops, another shopper disappears.
No one knows where? Only the smell of pork chops will tell the tale?

Dr. John T. Maddox

I graduated from Armstrong Atlantic State University with a BA in history in 1979. I graduated from Emory in 1988 with an MDIV. I graduated from St. Francis Bible College with a DD degree in 2011. I am an ordained elder of the South Georgia United Methodist Conference. I am an honorably discharged veteran of the US Navy (1970). I am married to Regina Maddox.

Prayer Warrior

Thank you Father for dedicated prayer warriors in Christ!
Through a sacrifice and continually touching others' lives!
Blessing others through agape love and care—
even when friends and enemies are not aware!
Thanks for your commitment, service and prayers!
 You are investing in others in a unique and loving way!
You are among those who listen, those who are
humble and those who are meek!
Praying for yourself and others is a worthy promise to keep!
Persevere through the sunshine and rain!
You are doing kingdom work, and there is no time to complain!
In the life of believers, prayer will remain!
Thanks for your dedication and praise!
We give glory, honor and to the heavenly Father our hands we raise!

Louise Bennett

My name is Louise Bennett, and I am humbled to be allowed to participate in the National Poetry Month celebration. I am a child of God, a mother, a wife, a friend, an employee, a sister, a daughter, a student, and a servant with purpose and plan. I write poetry to express and share with others the gift. I pray others are encouraged to journey on in kingdom's work! I was inspired to write this poem out of the opportunity and privilege of prayer as well as gratitude for prayer warriors in Christ. The poem is to recognize prayer warriors and give thanks for those who pray in faith, whether public or private.

Eyeward

Perhaps if the world were blind,
or could only see, the way we would
a sunset a stenciled life in a golden haze,
we wouldn't think to question
our days.

For those eyes
there is the sky, the life of sea and blossom,
the colors we see when the sun is high,
and we're left to admire the day.

But colors get washed away
like the exit to the world when it rains.
And there you are, safely out of reach and forever above,
and all we can do is imagine your efforts
to prove that you're more than a dream.

Here, in this broad spectrum of color
and light, where against, you should tower
but only become a gleam.
I bet you too, bulb and bloom, along endless fields,
forever seen but unseen.

Ryan Dieumegarde

It's Hard to Notice the Beauties

Seemed confident to the world: seye reh ni kaew tub
Seemed to believe in herself: seil tsuj erew esoht tub
What others saw: ees ton did ehs

What others thought: eb t'ndluoc thguoht ehs
That beautiful smile: dlrow eht morf sraet reh dih
That gleam in her eyes: lrig eht fo sraef eht dih

It's hard to look at oneself: swalf eht tsap kool dna

Brooke Harp

As an artist I love to write poetry, create pieces of art, and participate in the visual art of dance. I was inspired for this poem by the experiences in my life. I hope that this poem can reach out to others to help them realize how wonderful of a human being they are, no matter what others think or say.

You

The breeze through my hair reminds me of you.
Your touch so gentle,
Your hands so cold,
Your smile...so fragile.

Everything I see and hear reminds me of you.
Chocolate, your eyes
A kitten's meow, your voice
Music, your personality

What you don't know you'll never know
What you don't see you'll never see.

Abigail Johnson

Raised in the small town of Wayland, MI, I've grown up with many changes like any teenage girl has. I live with my mother and two other siblings. I write poetry when I need a stress reliever. Writing calms me down—cools my mind when I need it to be cooled.

Broken Hearts

Broken hearts
have missing space
fitting parts
are uncommon place
find that one,
that makes you whole
the answer to life
is that the goal?
a quest that many
will partake
but success
only a few will make
search the seas
scavenge the land
find that one
that makes life grand
feeling like
you're floating on air
returning to Earth
your only care
places to look
areas to go
everyone is on the search
to complete their soul.

Marcus Johnson

Initially this poem was intended for Ghenet. Someone very dear to me, she introduced me to a work by David McCord called Books Fall Open, and I wrote this poem in a similar form. I write poems as a means to vent out emotions for some people can bring about such powerful feelings that you were never aware of that you must find a way to lessen the effect of or else have them govern your mind and put you in an erratic state. Love truly makes you do crazy things and in doing these things you might find talents you would have never found had it not been for love. A being that never loved is a being that wasted potential.

Index

Abdulla, Munawwar 201
Aberle, Marilyn D. 277
Adams, Pamala D. 227
Aguirre, Geronimo 25
Aldridge, F. Le Vonier, II 57
Allen, Pamela S. 268
Anderson, Anastasia 105
Anderson, Jessica 289
Antall, Christine E. 209
Arana, Noemi 288
Arena, Patricia 293
Armstrong, Julie 269
Arrigo, Nicolette R. 218
Ashby, Garth R. 8
Atzert, Eleanor P. 249
Autry, Doris 79

Baker, Grace E. 18
Bangert, Gordon 160
Baramikova, Sadie 10
Barker, Alvin L. 26
Barnett, Gary L. 211
Bassett, Joan P. 47
Beier, Doris 207
Benjamin, Rhoda 34
Bennett, Louise 337
Bennin, Violet 261
Berry, Michelle L. 252
Best, Arnold 254
Blank, Keely 235
Bognar, Mary G. 285
Boyd, Aretha 49
Braley, Oleta P. 184
Brick, Florence M. 132
Brown, Aloyusis L. 103
Brown, Cleo E. 177
Burk, Laura J. 144
Butcher, Sierra N. 37

Cabrera, Josephine 14
Cacciotti, Joseph J. 175
Camp, Frances E. 225
Capps, Sondie Rae 54
Carpenter, Mark A. 113
Carrasco, Natane 197
Caskey, Lloyd D. 108
Casperson, Darby 309
Cecilio, Frances S. 85
Cervantes, Raquel G. 94
Chandler, Samantha 23
Chittum, Margaret 168
Ciesielski, Darcie 281
Cisneros, Norberto Franco 166
Cohen, Eileen Z. 217
Connolly, Rita 100
Cooper, Stephen 101
Copperwheat, Nathan 237
Craig, Arika L. 36
Craig, Stephanie 203
Crawford, Diane 51
Creed, Emily 311
Criez, Chloe 232
Cross, Ben 186
Cruze, Shirley K. 142
Cullen, Dick R. 139
Cunningham, Amber 162
Cunningham, Jennifer 191

Dalin, Karen 283
Daniels, Alexandria 134
Daniels, Sarah 107
Davidson, Amber 188
Davidson, Harry M. 274
Davis, Colt 127
DeGarmo, Tiffany A. 247
Degn, Mikayla 189
Deller, Faye A. 245
DeLoof, Danielle 314
Demicco, Joseph 307
Desmarais, Roger A. 331

Devilleres, David L. 55
Diaz, Maria M. 329
Dieumegarde, Ryan 338
Dillon, Charlotte M. 138
Dixon, Angelita J. 243
Doerr, Elmer 271
Dolan, Rebecca 320
Drilling, Steve 7
Dudley, Kayla 45
Dufour, Joey 9
Durden, Ciera 299
Duty, Dusty C. 42

Eckmann, Amanda L. 246
Eddington, Doris J. 92
Eldridge, Joseph 319
Ellis, Alisha 202
Emerson, Darcie 305
Emerson, Stephanie Bashein 242
Erikson, Carol A. 265

Fagan, Taylor Jene 133
Feigo, Alissa 126
Flannery, Bernice K. 226
Flostrand, Theela 74
Fogel, Deborah A. 40
Fredman, Joyce Helen 91
Fuchs, Seairra 135

Gabrielli, Anna Maria 6
Galipeau-Watson, Lorraine 326
Galvan, Ralph, Jr. 3
Gardner, Sherri Marie 84
Geist, Megan 129
Gentleman, Kuldip S. 270
Gilmore, Amethyst M. 52
Gladson, Jeannie H. 328
Glessner, Tyrone 38
Gudjoukova, Rada I. 99

Halder, Suresh C. 276
Haley, Teresa L. 24

Hall, Emalyn 12
Hall, Kristina 27
Hammonds, Clarence L. 223
Harp, Brooke 339
Harris, Emily 20
Hartley, Amber N. Burdette 164
Hatcher, Geraldine 287
Hellman-Lohr, Aisha 62
Henderson, Michael 136
Hendry-Vincent, Mandy Rae 161
Hobbs, Samantha 169
Holady, Ashley 248
Holloman, Teddy 158
Holloway, Annalecia 185
Howard-Oglesby, Pamela 30
Howell, Billy 104
Hudson, Billie S. 332
Huff, David 170
Humphrey, Verna R. 141
Hyatt, Ruby V. 267

Jaiswal, Pooja 120
Johnson, Abigail 340
Johnson, Douglas 125
Johnson, Emma 310
Johnson, Marcus 341
Johnson, Rachael 284
Johnson-Cooney, Terrence L. 212

Kavaldjiev, Kristin 323
King, Tisha A. 153
Konopka, Norma Marie 68
Kratz, Jason 87
Kremennaya, Veronika 128
Kriner, Harriet 266

Laclair, Mary 294
LaCount, Joshua 315
Lake, Eleanor 313
Landwehr, Russell 264
Laude, Julia 208
Lazaro, Roxana C. 279
Lee, Fred Thomas 228

Lefever, Grace T. 263
Leone, Robert 151
Levy, Maurice 33
Lima, Jutta E. 89
Liming, Paul 131
Livingston, Gary 194
Longcrier, Jonathan 122
Loomis, Rebecca 322
Lorilla, Adelfa G. 31
Love, Judy A. 159

Maddox, Dr. John T. 336
Mahon, Brianna V. 222
Manley, Anna E. 259
Marsden, Chelsea 199
Marshall, Courtney 198
Marshall, Natasha 233
Martin, Jessica 140
Martin, Rebecca L. 181
Martin, Sarah 302
Matros, Ron 333
Matthews, Kristy L. 67
Mattice, Phyllis J. 224
McKee, B. J. 2
McKenzie, Brianne 231
McKinnie, Briona Williams 123
McNeely, June L. 210
McPhail, Barbara J. 145
Mechenbier, Alyssa 137
Meckler, Nicki 291
Mendez, Luis 324
Michanczyk, Michael J., III 88
Miller, Lisa A. 213
Mireault, Lynn 236
Miszczak, Courtney 318
Molock, Tiffany J. 116
Molson, Daphne 76
Monroe, Cassi 148
Morgan, Jake 301
Mork, Beverly J. 286
Morrison, Anna L 335
Mosley, Lekeya 297
Myrick, Jocelyn 190

Nohilly, Michael 230

Orem, Sandra M. 262
Orr, Cache 300

Pagtakhan, Francisco 119
Parham, Julia 204
Parker, Queshia 110
Peacock, Kimberly 149
Peña, Melba 111
Peoples, Ardith L. 272
Perkins, Norma 72
Pickett, Farida 192
Pidlisny, Amanda 200
Plaster, Julian R. 334
Plys, Sierra 48
Pontious, Nancy L. 97
Posey, Glory 193
Powell, Julian 251

Quealy, Gerit 317
Quillen, De'Anna 220
Quill, Gwen Rose 238
Quinones, Eradia 65

Rand, Charles O. 174
Randeria, Bhupen V. 71
Rawn, Lorna F. 312
Ray, Pamela S. 29
Reed, Kelly 304
Reffalt, Mary J. 330
Reyes, Marisol A. 39
Richardson, Kellie 11
Robinson, Lori L. 32
Rodgers, Katherine 95
Rosenberger, Clara Mae 86
Rozenberg, Liza C. 93
Rubin, Carissa 244
Rutledge, Salena 130

Saiz, Frances 327
Salata, Tanya L. 70
Saleh, Carole 46
Samsami, David 143
Sanchez, Lori 13
Schlossman, Edward J. 216
Scroggins, Emily 43
Sellingsloh, Hulda K. 16
Shaw, Matthew C. 19
Sheffield, Linda 256
Shernock, Judith 83
Shibla, Devyn 296
Siefken, Rev. Burdetta 56
Siegel, Sami 308
Silva, Kathy 219
Smith, Carmella F. 215
Smith, Justin 156
Smith, Thomas L. 214
Solunac, Mihailo 171
Somerville, Jodi 121
Sommers, Robin C. 114
Soto, Lorena 180
Spaulding, Je'Nai 167
Spear, Bobby 206
Stirling, Louise 90
Straw, Becca 295
Sunner, Surinder 81

Taucher, Betty A. 325
Taylor, Meryl 60
Theobald, Holly S. 146
Tibbs, Florence C. 155
Traband, Elizabeth A. 112
Tucker, Mary 106
Tumey, Donna 282
Turrentine, Katherine 183

Uonelli, Elaine M. 275
Uphoff, Dr. Baron Joseph 63

Van Patten, Marilyn C. 173
VanDuren, Justin 306
Vega, JoGene 21

Velazquez, Martha 303
Vernon, Joy 124
Vides, Samantha 316
Vigneau, Patricia P. 109

Waddingham, Marina 147
Wahl, Ann 290
Walker, Emily 241
Walls, Joseph 82
Wassil, Kealy 250
Waters, Patina V. 50
Watts, Warren 292
Weaver, Helen 117
Weiner, Gary Stephen 187
Wells, Kelsey 273
White, Lewis A., Sr. 258
Williams, Rebecca 257
Williams, Walter Leon 78
Wilson, Lakin 150
Wilson, Pennee 260
Winters, Brenda Kay 1
Wolfe, Iva 59
Wolters, Sarah Carleton 77
Worsley, Alexis 196

Yanushevskaya, Ella 255
Yeager, Edward S. 152
Young, Meghan 229

Zemp, G. LaWayne 98
Zieman, Natalina 240

CPSIA information can be obtained at www.ICGtesting.com
Printed in the USA
BVOW080117270712

296305BV00003B/1/P